THE ULTIMATE SMART GIRL'S GUIDE

advice about friends, family, school, sports, and more!

Dear Reader,

Growing up can be exciting. It can also be confusing. Lots of things keep changing in your life: your body, your feelings, your family, your school, and your friends. You've got new responsibilities and new ambitions. Some days you wake up feeling ready for any challenge, and some days you feel overwhelmed by the simplest task.

Life is full of changes. The way you face them is part of what makes you *you*. The grown-ups in your life went through many of the changes you're experiencing. Your parents and other trusted adults are a smart source of information and encouragement. Sharing your thoughts and feelings with them is always a good idea.

Finding answers for yourself is a good idea, too. This book is full of advice on getting along with your family and friends, being your best at school, exploring new hobbies, and navigating the changing world around you. You'll learn how to nourish your mind, body, and spirit.

Never stop growing!

Your friends at American Girl

contents

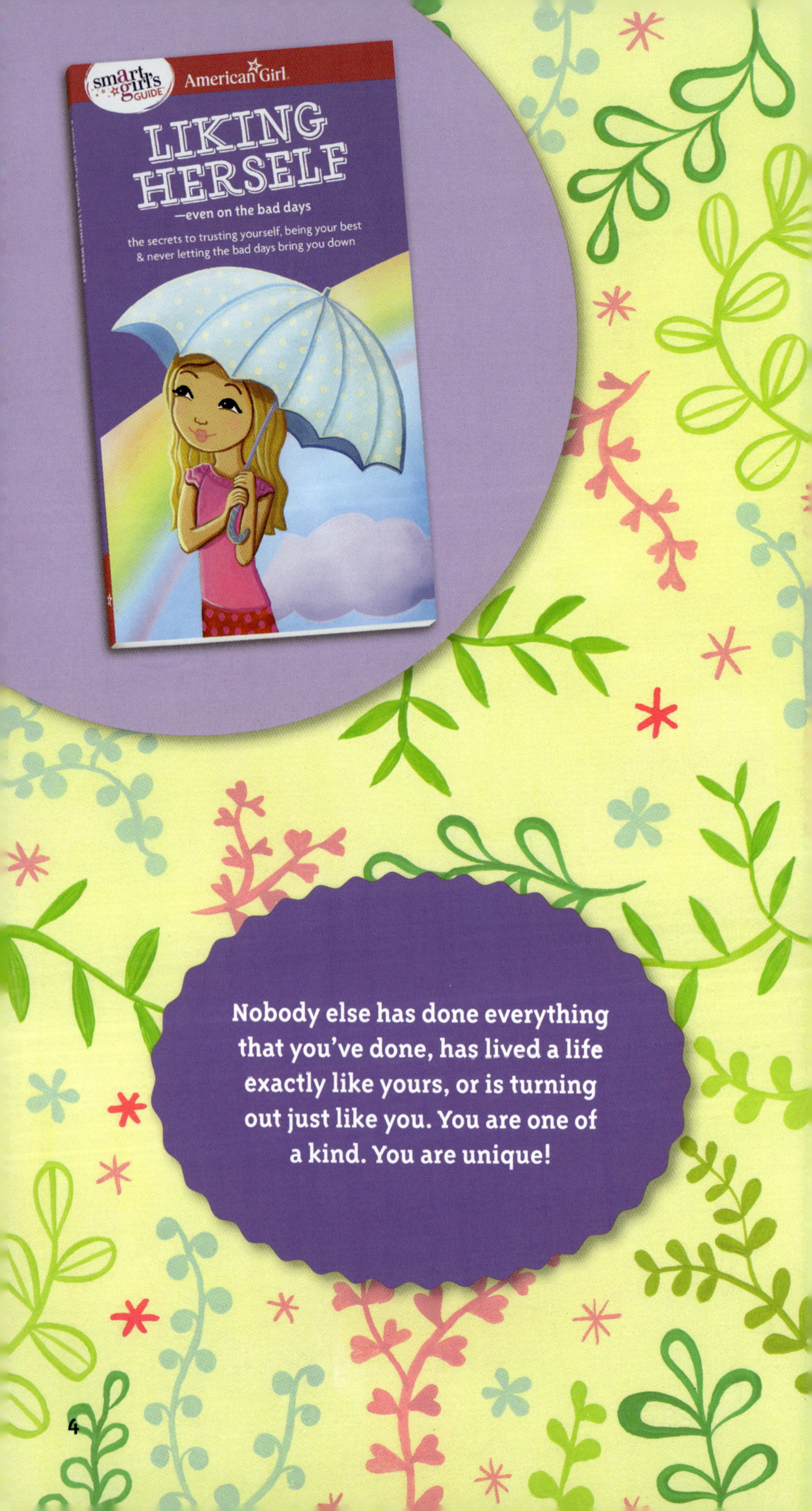

Nobody else has done everything that you've done, has lived a life exactly like yours, or is turning out just like you. You are one of a kind. You are unique!

it's all about you . . .

once upon a time . . .

When you were a baby, you were so cute and tiny. Your parents paid a lot of attention to you and took care of everything you needed. Life was pretty easy for you then.

Then you learned to crawl. You could decide where you wanted to go and even reach for some things by yourself.

You started to separate from your parents and make friends away from home. You were learning to make your own choices and figuring out what you liked and didn't like.

Your day was filled with lots of learning and responsibility. Besides schoolwork, you were also figuring out things about other kids—such as who were like you and who were different. And those kids were learning about you, too!

Now it's sometimes hard to figure out where you belong and which kids to hang out with. You may try out a few groups before you decide where you feel comfortable.

Your body is changing, and you're not used to it. You knew it would happen one day, but so much is going on that you feel a little confused. Everyone wishes she could wave a magic wand and choose for herself just how and when her body changes, but that's not the way it works. These physical changes just happen automatically, no matter what you wish for.

you've changed—and that's a good thing!

You might feel self-conscious about the outward changes. But even though you're getting taller and your body is starting to look more grown-up, exciting things are happening inside, too! You're getting better at skills that were once hard for you. You're aware of things you hadn't noticed before, and you care about different things. That's the way it's supposed to be!

Change may seem scary, but without it you'd still be a tiny baby being taken care of by your parents. Some days that may sound great, but what about all the cool things you've done so far that you'd miss out on?

In the space below, list the things that are great about being who you are now:

emotions change, too

Your brain and hormones are sending your body signals to grow in special ways, which might make you feel different than you've felt before. It's important to recognize what you're feeling and learn how to understand or change your emotions when you need to.

Sad: You're down in the dumps and don't see a quick way to feel better. Your eyes are teary, and you feel too tired to smile at things you usually think are funny.

Angry: You have so much energy inside that you feel like yelling or squeezing something. It could even feel like you might explode. Usually this feeling comes when something happens that you think shouldn't have happened.

Worried: You're scared and nervous that something bad is about to happen, and you can't get the idea out of your head. You might have a headache or stomachache. Another word for this feeling is *anxious.*

Paranoid: You keep expecting something bad to happen and spend all your time watching for signs that it is coming. Even when everything is OK, you think you see clues that things are going to be bad, so you are always on your guard.

Embarrassed: You feel as if everyone is looking and laughing at you for something you did wrong. Your face might turn red and hot and your body might get sweaty. You wish you could snap your fingers and disappear.

Exaggerating the truth

Even the happiest and most self-confident people feel negative emotions once in a while. **Being sad, angry, worried, paranoid, or embarrassed is simply part of life.** However, when your self-esteem is low, these emotions may occur more often, possibly causing you to say mean things to yourself. Doctors who know about behavior call this **distortion,** which means that your mind exaggerates the facts and makes a situation seem worse than it is. It's like looking at something with a **magnifying glass**—everything looks big when it's actually really small.

Distortion happens when something doesn't seem to make sense. For example, if you don't like your hair because you think it's frizzy and then a classmate says she wishes she had hair just like yours, you might not think it is true or think she is being sarcastic. Your brain wants only information that matches the way you already feel. If it doesn't match, your brain has to figure out the truth. If your self-esteem is really low, your brain will distort what your classmate said and find a way to make her words seem like a lie, so that it fits the bad image you already have of yourself.

If you want to **boost your self-esteem,** then you must convince your brain that what the girl said is really true. When you challenge a distortion enough times, it goes away and you see the facts through a normal lens.

It's really a mind game. When your self-esteem is low, your old way of thinking keeps winning because your brain wants to keep things as they are. But with some practice in fighting that distortion, your **good self-image can take the lead.**

Brain games

Think of your brain messages as if they are TV shows: One show features laughter and smiling people, and another is full of insults and mean people. If you want to feel happy, which show would you watch? The first one, of course! It's the same with your self-talk. The messages you play in your brain affect how you feel. If you fill up on positive thoughts, you'll more likely **feel positive about yourself.** But stock up on negative talk, and you're probably not going to feel great about yourself.

Brain A:
So you have a zit on your face. No sweat. Everyone gets them. With the great hair day you're having and the new sweater you're wearing, no one will even notice that itty-bitty, teeny-tiny blemish. And if they do, who cares? Make a joke about it. "Anyone for a game of connect the dots?" Laugh it off and move on. People will admire your carefree attitude!

Brain B:
You're so ugly. Just look at that gigantic zit on your face! Everyone is looking right at it. If your mom doesn't let you stay home from school this week, then you'd better think about wearing a paper bag over your head until it goes away. You don't want to scare everyone, do you?

retrain your brain

When your mind goes into magnifying-glass mode and negative self-talk is all you hear, **set your brain straight.**

Step one: It's not what you think

Remember that . . .

- other people really don't look at you as closely as you look at yourself. In fact, they're probably hoping that you don't notice things they're stressing about.
- almost nothing lasts forever. What people notice or say today may just as quickly be forgotten tomorrow.
- what you're noticing now is only a tiny part of you. All the other parts you like are still there.
- spending less time thinking about bad things leaves more time for fun stuff.
- by next week, you'll hardly remember why you had a bad day today.

Step two: Change the channel

If you don't like feeling down in the dumps, change the channel in your mind. Doing something different can help shift your focus from the negatives to the positives.

Here are some ideas.

- Dance to a peppy **song.**
- Play a **board game** with your little sister.
- Make a **card** for your mom.
- Invite a friend over to watch a **movie.**
- Read a **book.**
- **Clean** your room.
- Bake some **cookies** with your dad.
- Make **place cards** to put at the table for your next family meal.
- Invent new ways to **sign your name.**
- Invent a **tongue twister** you can teach your friends.
- Practice **writing** with your other hand.
- **Memorize** the alphabet backward.
- Plant some **seeds** in an empty egg carton.

Step three: Look for the positive in yourself

Answer these questions to discover what you really think and feel.

- What positive word best describes you?
- What makes you different from everyone you know?
- What is your dream job?
- What's the bravest thing you've ever done?
- Name one thing you can do to cheer up whenever you're feeling blue.
- Which family memory always makes you smile?
- What outdoor activity do you love doing?
- Who inspires you to be your best?

smart girl's GUIDE
American Girl
UNDERSTANDING FAMILIES
feelings, fighting & figuring it out

get close . . . and closer!

The secret to getting closer to your family is being curious about their stories, their dreams, and their hearts. Have fun together! Here are some activities you can do that will make you smile—and help you get to know one another even better.

family fun facts

How well do you know your family? Complete the sentences below by circling a family member and filling in the blank. Next, become a reporter. Interview your family members to see how many of the questions you answered right.

1. One of my parent's favorite books is ______________________________.

2. My sibling's favorite room in our house is ______________________________.

3. One of my parent's favorite movies is ______________________________.

4. When my grandmother/grandfather was a child, she/he lived in ______________________________.

5. When my other grandmother/grandfather was a child, she/he lived in ______________________________.

6. At my age, my parent wanted to be a ______________________________ when she/he grew up.

7. If my sibling could travel anywhere in the world, it would be ______________________________.

8. One of the biggest adventures my parent ever had was ______________________________.

9. One of my parent's closest friends is named ______________________________.

10. My sibling's best part of the day is ______________________________.

11. My parent's favorite kind of music is ______________________________.

Scoring

9 or more correct
Congratulations! You listen closely to the people in your family. If knowing fun facts about your family were a contest, you'd win first prize!

5–8 correct
You've been doing a good job paying attention to details in your family. With a little work, you'll know all your family trivia!

4 or fewer correct
There's a whole world of fun family facts out there to discover. The more you know about your family members, the better you'll understand them—and that can mean more closeness and good times at home.

Celebrate your specialness! Every family member has quirks. Strange as it sounds, those are the things that can make families closer.

My dad is a terrible singer. When he sings, my sister and I start singing as loud as we can so we can't hear him, but then he sings louder. Then my mom starts yelling at us all to be quiet. The weird thing is we do this every day!

—Madeline, age 11

Our dog, Rusty, makes this barky sound, and my mom talks back to him. Then he talks back to her. They even talk about the weather!

—Annie, age 10

My mom gets excited over nothing. Today she started dancing because she got a book about flowers. It was crazy.

—Kellye, age 12

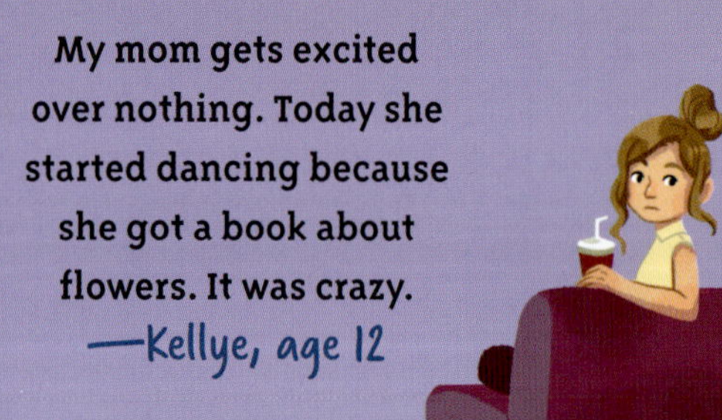

My aunt always says, "Cute, cute, cute!" when she likes something. She says it three times, never once or twice—always three.

—Rhonda, age 11

Enjoy the nighttime neighborhood. If you live in a place where you can walk at night, ask your family to take an evening stroll. The world feels totally different in the dark, and there's a special closeness that comes from seeing your street at bedtime. Besides, a walk in the evening is a good time for sharing stories of the day or memories from the past. Don't forget a flashlight!

Share your dreams. When you wake up, tell the story of your dream to a parent or sibling quickly, before you forget. Does anybody in your family have ideas about what your dream might mean? Are there clues in the dream that can help you solve a daytime problem? If morning is too busy, write down your dream and share it in the evening. Ask your family what they dreamed about, too!

Join family members while they do something they love. Watch hockey with your brother, or listen to jazz with your mom. Make dinner or hit golf balls with your dad. Even if it's not your favorite thing to do, it will draw you closer. Maybe next time, they'll do what you love to do—with you!

Play "Best Thing, Worst Thing." At the dinner table, ask each person to tell the best thing that happened that day. Then ask each person to tell the worst part of his or her day. If people are in a joking mood, have a contest to see who had the very best and very worst days. If your family is feeling serious, simply share your stories. Either way, you'll feel closer than you did before!

Get a game going. Talk with your family about regularly setting aside an evening to play games. You could call it Find Family Fun Night! On FFF Night, turn off computers, the TV, and phones, and break out a game. Teach a younger sibling how to play something new. Other times, choose a game based on luck so that even little sibs will have a chance to win.

Play by the numbers. Grab any family member, or divide your family into two teams. Write the list below on another sheet of paper so that you have two copies. Yell, "One, two, three—go!" and see which team can find the answers most quickly.

When you're done, see if both teams got the same answers. The team with the most correct answers gets to take the other team out for ice cream!

Get tangled up in love. Find a ball of yarn or string. Ask your family to stand in a circle. Start by holding the end of the string and tossing the ball to someone else. (It will unwind as you toss it.) After you toss the ball, say something good about the person who caught it.

Next, have the catcher toss the ball to someone else—still holding on to part of the string—and say what he or she appreciates about that person. Keep tossing the ball around the circle until the string is all unwound. What a web of good feelings you made!

Plant memories. Plant a tree or a bush together to mark a family event. Graduating from elementary school? That's a big event. Anniversaries and birthdays are, too. So are sad times such as losing a grandparent. Your family will feel connected on the day you plant the tree and when you see it throughout the year.

Send signals. Speak your own private language by making up family-only code words or signals. A tug on your ear could mean "Look at that." Saying "FHB" when guests are over for dinner could be code for "Family, hold back" so that there will be plenty of food for guests. But be careful about using family signals in public. They can give you incurable giggles!

Make it official. Schools have official songs. States have official birds. Why not your family? Brainstorm with other family members to fill in the blanks below:

Family song: ______________________________

Family mascot: ______________________________

Family food: ______________________________

Family cheer: ______________________________

____

____

Family color: ______________________________

Family bird: ______________________________

Draw your family flag here.
(Include symbols, words, and colors that represent your family to you.)

Look into the future. Make a list of things that are true right now about you and your family. You can also make predictions for the coming year. Seal the list in an envelope marked "Open Next Year." Pack it away with the holiday decorations. Read the list together next year to see how things have changed!

Share a read. Have you read a good book recently? Your family might enjoy lots of the books you like, too. Loan a book to your mom, dad, sister, or brother. Talk about the plot twists, and compare what you thought. ("Could you believe the ending?" "What would you have done in her place?" "I cried in that part, too.")

Cheer for the home team. What are the biggest challenges your family members are going through? Is your brother having a hard time with math? Has your mom been spending long hours working? Leave a note cheering him or her on. Knowing that you believe in them will help your family members face their troubles and reach their goals.

smart girl's GUIDE
American Girl
WORRY
how to feel less stressed and have more fun
BFF
I probably spend half
my life worrying.
—Savannah
21

all stressed out

tied up in knots

Worries. We all have them. Some are mild. Some are strong. Sometimes they show up one by one. Other times they may start pouring in so fast you think there's nothing you could ever do to stop them.

Call it nerves, call it anxiety, or call it being stressed out. When worry has you tangled up in knots, it may seem as if no one could possibly understand how it feels.

Not so. There are girls all around who know exactly how it feels because the truth is, a lot of girls struggle with worry.

why all the worry?

Experts say kids worry more these days than in the past. It's not hard to see why.

Life is packed.

School, piano lessons, soccer matches, clubs, mathalons, performances, family events. You're forever rushing off to do the next thing. Chances are, even if you're alone in your room, things are hopping. Phones ring. Texts ping in. Nothing ever settles down. It's hard to relax.

The pressure's on.

School is more demanding. There's more homework, more classes, more teachers—and more pressure to do well. And that's not to mention the pressure to do well in sports and other areas of life. *Argh!*

Life is changing.

Friendships can be complicated. There's more drama, more gossip, more tension in the lunchroom. At the same time, your body is changing. The "you" you are today may not feel at *all* like the one you were last year. Lots of girls worry about what comes next. *Will my breasts start growing soon? What if my period starts in the middle of dance class?* Your body will do exactly what it's supposed to, but it will have its own unpredictable timetable.

Your world is getting bigger.

You are building your independence. More and more, you're venturing out of the cozy cocoon your parents watched over when you were little. You're deciding more things for yourself. It's exciting, but a bit scary. You're not always certain what to do.

Things feel less safe.

Weather disasters, wars in distant countries, unsafe schools. Bad news can be worrisome even for adults. For kids who are just beginning to pay attention, it may be plain scary. What kind of world are you stepping into anyway?

There are always problems.

Of course, there are plenty of things closer to home that a girl might have good reason to worry about, too. One girl may have a loved one who's sick. Another may be anxious about arguments in the family. Money problems. Marriage problems. Every girl has some family concerns on her list. And as if that weren't enough . . .

Worry can be contagious.

If adults or others around her tend to worry about things, a girl can pick up the worry habit. A girl whose aunt shrinks from meeting new people, or whose dad is too frightened to fly on airplanes, might learn to be anxious—not only about those specific things but about other things, too.

Add it up.

A day has only 24 hours, but for a lot of girls that means a bajillion opportunities to worry about *something*.

when you worry

Anxiety is normal. It's your brain and body's built-in alarm system, and it has only one job: to protect you. Back when humans wore animal hides and lived in caves, this alarm system helped your ancestors escape from hungry animals.

When something sets off the alarm, anxiety gets you ready to . . .

fight back or **freeze so you won't be noticed** or **run away.**

To do this, anxiety affects you in three ways.

1. Anxiety focuses **your thoughts** on the danger. *I've got to get away!* Suddenly, you can't think of anything else. Not. One. Single. Other. Thing.

2. Anxiety revs up your body and changes **how you feel.** Your heart beats faster and your muscles tense up. Is your skin sweaty? Is your stomach tied in knots? Do your legs feel like rubber bands? That's anxiety at work, too.

3. Anxiety can affect **what you do** in an instant. A heartbeat ago, you were strolling through the woods, humming along to your favorite song. And now you are . . . running wild!

The anxiety alarm can still kick in even if you're not fleeing wild animals. An ordinary thing like a visit to the dentist can set it off if you're worried enough. And the science test Mr. Baake is giving—the one that counts for a third of your grade? Or the party your karate teammate is throwing—where you're sure you won't know a soul? Those could trip the alarm, too.

Anxiety is your own personal bodyguard. It rallies to keep you safe from anything that's scary to *you.*

worry words
When you hear these words inside your head, it's a red flag. Your worries are talking, and you're right to be suspicious.
never
always
no one
can't
nothing
everyone
should
impossible
supposed to
ought to
have to
shouldn't

Worries that spread

If you allow a goal in gym class, do you automatically think that other things will go wrong, too?

Now nothing will go right.
I always mess up.

If friend A is mad at you, are you convinced that friends B through Z are mad, too?

Everyone thinks I'm wrong!
No one takes my side!

Thoughts like these let a problem in one area of your life spill over into places where it doesn't belong. To fix this mistake, try drawing a mental line around the problem. Tell yourself: "Just because I didn't play well today doesn't mean I won't do OK on the math quiz."

All-or-nothing thinking

It's impossible to finish this assignment.
Leila never sits with me.

All-or-nothing thoughts like these can really supercharge worries. Chances are, the truth is less black and white. An assignment might not be easy, but it's probably not impossible. And maybe Leila sits with Carmen on Wednesdays because they've just had gym together, just as she sits with you on Thursdays after the two of you get out of band. Try to find the middle ground. Using words like "sometimes" (instead of "always" or "never") or "challenging" (instead of "impossible") can help you think about things in a less stressful way.

Rules and more rules

I have to get all A's in English.
I should have learned a handspring by now.

Rule-bound thoughts tell you there's only one way for you to be OK. They tell you that if things don't happen exactly the way they're supposed to, it will be a disaster. If that were true, who *wouldn't* worry? The truth is that you're still learning and growing, discovering who you are and what you can do. There are an infinite number of ways things can go and still turn out right for you. Go easier on yourself by thinking about your goals in a gentler way. "I'd like to . . ." "I want to . . ." "It would be nice if . . ." are great places to start.

go, fight, win!

No girl likes the way she feels when she's worried or afraid. But anxiety isn't *all* bad.

When worry focuses your thoughts, it can help you zero in on anything that's really important at home or school. When it revs up your body, it can give you a burst of energy.

The good thing about worry is that it can push you to do what needs to get done.

Get busy!

Stay focused!

Do your best!

So when you're worried, maybe you can put those feelings to use. Try asking yourself: "What, exactly, is nagging at me? Is there something I can do about it?"

If you feel like you ate a bowl of butterflies two days before the Spanish vocabulary quiz, that feeling might be telling you to put away your tablet and get out the flash cards. That headache you get whenever you think about your piano recital or a swim meet might be reminding you to practice a little more, try a little harder.

If there's something you *can* do about what's worrying you, the surest cure is to just do it. Now. If worry can get you going, it's on your side.

Remember kindergarten? Back then, friendships were pretty easy. Your parents arranged your playdates. If you and your friend had a fight about who got the cherry lollipop, an adult stepped in and calmed things down.

all about friends

Now you're older, and a lot's changed. You're choosing your own friends and trying to solve your own problems. You need more from your friends, and they need more from you.

You've learned that a true friendship is a two-way street, and that both people have to work to make a relationship a success. You listen to your friend when she's having a bad day, and she does the same for you. Neither one of you is "in charge." You're equal. You can compromise when you need to, and you both know that your opinions matter.

Every friendship is a little different. You may value one girl for the way she makes you laugh when you're down. You may value another for the way she helps you solve problems. Underneath it all, though, the best friendships share some very basic things.

what makes a great friend?

What some girls say:

"A really good friend has to be able to understand you and the way you think, appreciate you for who you are, and always keep your secrets. When a friend lies, it can ruin a friendship for a long time."

"A real friend sticks up for you in tough situations."

"A friend should be someone you are comfortable with—not someone who you are afraid will laugh at you."

"I like a friend who is nice, truthful, and fun to be with. Also creative, so we are never bored."

"A true friend doesn't get mad at every little thing."

"I think a real friend is someone who likes you for who you are. My best friend is more popular than I am and has a lot more friends than I do. She has so many other choices, but she picked me because she likes me."

"Someone who will encourage me."

"A friend is dependable and doesn't just say she will be there and not show up. It's a trust thing."

What you say

Think about it. What do you think makes a great friend? On a piece of paper, make a list of qualities that a girl should have to be one of your good friends. Put a ☆ next to the things you can't do without.

true friend test

Good friends are good for you. How do your buddies measure up? Picture each girl in your mind and ask yourself whether these statements are true or not.

After we're together, I feel happy and good about myself.

yes no

When something good happens, she's the first one I want to tell, because I know she'll be really excited for me.

yes no

When I'm angry about something and just need to talk, she'll listen.

yes no

When I say, "OK, we'll do it your way," it doesn't feel like I'm giving in, because chances are that the last time we disagreed, she did things my way.

yes no

She brings out the best in me.

yes no

We never run out of things to talk about.

yes no

When she's sad or upset, I feel bad and want to help in any way I can.

yes no

I can make a total fool of myself, and she won't cut me down for it.

yes no

I would stand up for her, and I know she'd do the same for me.

yes no

We can sit and work on a project or watch TV and not say a word—it never feels awkward.

yes no

answer:

The girl who inspires you to say yes to these statements is a friend through and through. **Hold on to her.**

And the others? Well, it's the rare friendship that's absolutely perfect. But answering no many times is not a good sign. Just because you've been friends with a girl for a long time or because you spend a lot of time together doesn't mean a friendship is true-blue.

Friendship File

Lydia

Lydia is spunky and creative. She loves to speak her mind, and she loves to help people. She hangs out with four or five other girls at school. When tragedy struck Lydia's family, she turned to her friends.

What happened

Lydia loves and admires her brother, Randy, who is two years older. Randy injured his spine diving into shallow water at a lake. He lost the use of his legs and had to learn to use a wheelchair. His accident hit her hard—really hard.

Lydia felt so sad and scared that she hardly knew what to do. Sometimes she shared these feelings with her parents, but she knew that they were hurting, too. She didn't want to add to their worries. So she carried her grief to school and talked with her friends. Sometimes they listened, but they didn't say much. Lydia could see that her friends felt awkward. It was like they just didn't get it. After a while, she stopped talking about her brother and pretended that everything was fine.

But it wasn't fine. Lydia needed to feel close to someone. She got clingy. She would try to be involved in every conversation that took place, be a part of everything that was going on. She remembers, "I was totally hyper—I was terrified of being left out!" But that's just what happened. Annoyed by Lydia's neediness, the other girls kicked her out of the group. They even wrote a long list of "annoying things about Lydia" and gave it to her. So just when she thought the situation couldn't get any worse, it did.

What she did

Lydia was heartbroken. She spent more time at home, holding tight to her family. She cried a lot. When she became, as she says, "mad as all get-out," she'd write songs and play them on the piano or the violin. Music really helped.

After a few weeks, Lydia struck up a conversation with a girl named Grace. Grace sat in the back of the classroom and kept mostly to herself. Lydia had hardly noticed her before. Now the two hit it off and started to hang out together. Before long they were inseparable. Lydia remembers, "Grace never got tired of me." Lydia joked that Grace was an "angel" sent to help. And Grace did help. She stuck it out with Lydia during that whole awful time. When Lydia ranted about people who didn't have a disability but parked in the accessible parking spaces, Grace listened. And when Lydia could do nothing but cry as she watched her brother struggle, Grace was there. One day when Grace knew Lydia was feeling really down, she showed up with two pink roses, just to say she cared.

How it worked out

As Lydia's family adjusted and accepted their new challenges, Lydia's life grew more stable. Today, Grace remains one of Lydia's best friends. The old group? Well, they eventually started being nice to Lydia again. She gets along with them, but it will never be the same. She looks back now and says, "They're not bad people. They just had no idea what the true meaning of friendship is, and I guess I didn't, either." But she does now. She absolutely does.

respect

You've heard the word your whole life—at home, in school, everywhere: respect. "Respect adults," "Respect yourself," "Respect the rules," "Be respectful," and so on.

So what does respect have to do with friendship? Everything.

Respect

Respect is what you offer a friend because you honor the friendship.

Friendship

You could treat a friend rudely—nobody's going to give you detention or ground you if you do. But you choose not to do that. You want your friend to know how much she means to you. Of all the things that can bind two people together, respect may be the strongest.

Having respect for someone else means

- resisting the temptation to talk about your friend behind her back, even when you're angry.
- trusting that her intentions are good ones.
- believing her when she says she's sorry.
- being happy for her even when you're really jealous.

Showing a friend respect takes effort—but it's worth it. With trust and respect, you and your friend will have fewer problems, solve them more easily, and enjoy each other a whole lot more.

friendship hot spots

So you've found a great friend. She has all the qualities you value most, and in so many ways she's perfect. That's it. **Right?**

Uh-uh. It's not that easy. Friendships need care every bit as much as that flower in the garden needs water. Even the best of friends have problems now and again. Maybe your feelings are hurt because your friend walked home with someone else when you expected her to walk with you. Maybe you're annoyed because she calls ten times a night. Maybe you're jealous of her big success, or she's jealous of yours. It isn't as if your friendship is in doubt, really, but things aren't so wonderful, either.

You've hit a friendship hot spot. It's probably not a big deal: a lot of trouble comes from mistakes and miscommunication. But even a little problem can rub and rub like a stone in your shoe until it makes a real sore. **The time to deal with it is now.**

best friends?

A best friend can be as comforting as a cup of hot cocoa on a cold winter's night. She listens, she keeps your secrets, and when you're together, it just feels right. You feel safe and secure knowing she's there when you need her.

But there may be times when having a best friend makes you feel tied down. Do you always need to sit with her at the movies? Can you never be partners with someone new? What if you want to be close with another girl, too? Is that OK? What if your best friend feels angry or jealous? What do you do?

Are best friends a good idea or a bad one?

It depends. For some girls, having a best friend feels like too much pressure. For others, it's the only way to go. If that's you, here are two things to remember.

One: Don't get into a tight relationship with just anybody. If you can't be yourself with a girl, then proclaiming yourselves "best friends" isn't a good idea. It's better to let your friendship grow for a while. If you want to get closer, work on the little conflicts that come along. Let her know what you enjoy about her friendship and what you would like to see change.

Two: Even best friends aren't best friends every single day. Friendships are like a dance. You get close for a while, then you pull away, and then you get close again. That's normal. Keep talking to your friend when you're feeling more distant, but be sure you have other friends, too. Never put all your energy into a single friendship. That way, if you and your best friend aren't doing well this week, you aren't left out in the cold. In the end, that means a lot less pressure on the friendship.

Don't get me started.
My school is the biggest place
for drama. There's schoolwork—tests,
homework, classes. There's dating. Who's
in and out. The feeling that other people
are against you. Some days I feel like
the whole world is watching me look
for a place to sit. It's not fun.

—American Actress

feelings rule

emotional overload

Uh-oh.

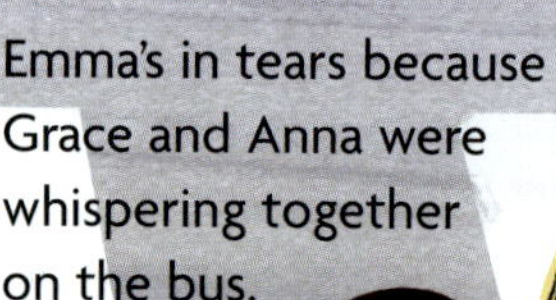

Emma's in tears because Grace and Anna were whispering together on the bus.

Katie sent a mean text to Maya from Liam's phone. Maya yelled at him in the hall.

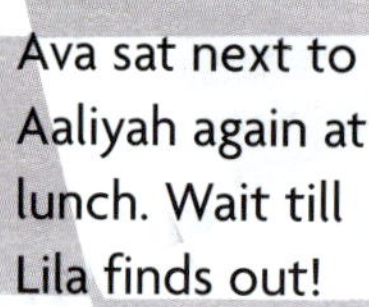

Ava sat next to Aaliyah again at lunch. Wait till Lila finds out!

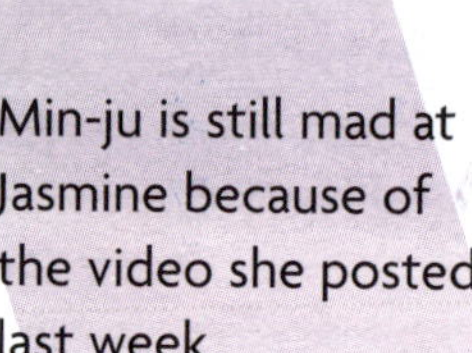

Min-ju is still mad at Jasmine because of the video she posted last week.

Three hours after Bianca broke up with Jason, Rachel was talking with him at the bus stop. Now all the soccer girls are saying mean stuff about Rachel online.

Olivia is talking a mile a minute. Is she happy? Is she mad? You don't know. But she's excited, that's for sure.

What's going on here?

It seems like everyone's always excited about something. A problem that starts between two people suddenly involves five. Then twenty. One crisis dies down and the next one starts. There are days you'd rather stay in bed with the cat than get up and deal with it all.

People use the word "drama" to describe making a big deal out of something small and silly. But no conflict seems small when you're dragged into it. Drama can change how friends treat friends. It can change how you feel about yourself. The fact is, living with daily drama is a very big deal indeed.

tears and fears

I hate puberty! I've got so many emotions and I can't control them. I feel like my world is falling apart. Help!
—Kidnapped by Puberty

You're not alone! Most kids feel torn up by emotions during puberty, and science says there's a very good reason for that.

In puberty, a girl's body produces chemicals called hormones. These hormones create physical changes that are easy to see, like growing taller and getting curvier. What you don't see is that those same hormones are also at work on your emotions. The structure of your brain is changing. The way your nervous system works is changing. These emotional changes are not as obvious as the physical ones, but they are every bit as real.

chemical changes inside the body =

Intense Emotions

and

MOOD SWINGS

With all these changes happening at once, a girl can feel pretty confused. Chances are, you've never been so aware of your body in your entire life—or so worried about how others see you. You compare yourself with your friends. You might compare yourself with stars on social media. Lots of girls become their own worst critics.

Getting ready in the morning used to take you five minutes. Now your dad has to knock on the bathroom door to get you away from the mirror. You may have days when you walk around all day afraid of the moment someone points a finger at a flaw you're trying to hide. School feels different. You don't want to stick out. You try hard not to make mistakes and to save face when you do.

Along the way, you may start feeling like "you" is just a part you're playing. You're changing so fast. Who can tell who you are anymore, anyway?

experiments

Who are you? How do you fit in? Who do you want to be? Now that your body is reinventing itself, you may think it's a great chance to reinvent yourself in other ways, too.

In some ways, it's all a big experiment. Does this shirt seem like you? What music do you want to hear? Do you really want to move up in soccer, or would you rather switch it up and play more tennis? A few years ago, your parents would have made a lot of these decisions. Now many of them are up to you.

You are also exploring those big, new emotions knocking around in your chest. Why can't you stop thinking about that kid you have a crush on? Why did that group chat have you crying in the bathroom over lunch? You're not quite sure.

The fact is, everybody around you is struggling with the same feelings and changes that you are. Friendships are shifting constantly, and you're all keeping track of the results.

Is Chloe getting popular? Is Maddy into hockey? Is Leah sitting with the nerds? And what about you? Do you want to hang out with your new pals from band or the friends you've had since second grade? Do you feel closer to Maria or to Layla? And does Layla feel closer to you or to Kate?

School is harder. Activities are intense. Put it in a pot and turn the heat on high. What do you get?

what drama means for you

Living in constant crisis asks all you can give and then some.

Waste of time

The trouble between Zoey and Aria has been going on for three days straight. It's a full-time job keeping up. You finally managed to settle down to work on your presentation, but every time you get an idea, another text pings in.

Your friends' quarrel is eating up your life. You're getting less sleep at night and less done during the day, and the emotional ups and downs can be exhausting. You could be learning to dance, working at a soup kitchen, or biking around the lake. Instead you're caught up in a problem that you can't really do much about and that doesn't directly involve you.

Shades of Gray

Yesterday, you told Jaycee your secret. Now she's told it to Taylor. Jaycee has ruined your life.

Strong feelings—feelings like anger, fear, and sadness—can be so overwhelming that the world looks black-and-white. People and events seem either very, very right or very, very wrong. But in real life not every problem is a catastrophe, and a friend who's made a mistake isn't terrible (you make mistakes, too!). When you have a problem with a friend, you need to think and plan in order to fix it. Does overreacting help? Just the opposite.

Drama = more drama

One minute you're upset with your friend Ashley. The next you're grounded for yelling at your little sister. Your brother calls you Hurricane Hannah, and in your heart of hearts you do feel sort of like a disaster.

Moods are hard to shake. If you're mad, hurt, and anxious at school, chances are you're going to be mad, hurt, and anxious when you walk in the door at home. Problems with friends can create problems at home, and problems at home can create problems with friends.

Less trust

Last month, Sophia decided she didn't like Amber and said you should stop liking Amber, too. Today Sophia said a bunch of bad stuff about Saskia. What if Sophia decides to stop liking Saskia?

Excluding kids hurts the person who's left out, but that's not all it does. In instances like this, a single girl can poison an entire friend group by creating an atmosphere of fear and shame. Friends who should be open and free with one another get guarded. There's more plotting and planning. There's less trust. There's less truth. What you share becomes the exact opposite of what we all want from the word "friendship."

Lonely

When you're with your friends, you feel fake.

It's natural for a girl to try on different clothes, different ideas, and different ways of expressing herself. There's a little bit of acting mixed up with that, which is perfectly natural, too. It's about discovering who you are and what kind of person you want to become. The problem is that many girls are nervous about what other people think. When emotions run high, they might end up worrying more about how they *appear* than how they truly *are* and what they truly feel. That can make a person feel empty—and lonely, even among friends.

rewrite the script

People may think drama is inevitable. It isn't.
Girls like you can rewrite the script.

I don't need a lot of drama.
I can make different choices.
I can rewrite the script.

I know that other kids are like me. Everybody wants to fit in some-where. Everybody's trying hard to be liked and to figure out what sort of person she wants to be.

It's best to be fair. I don't want to overreact or exaggerate. When I'm upset about something, I try to calm down before I act.

I'm going to try new things, but I'll decide for myself what works best for me. I'm not going to change to suit someone else.

I have strong feelings, just like most kids. My feelings aren't good or bad. They just are. I feel them. I'm not going to pretend I don't. But I will work to control them. I don't want them to control me.

I believe in doing what's right. I'm going to make some mistakes. Everybody does. But I will never stop trying to be a decent person. I'm going to grow up liking myself.

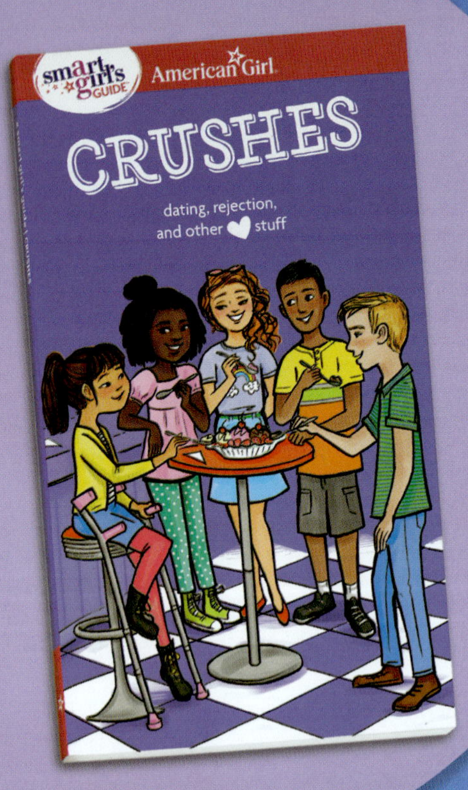

Lots of kids—boys and girls alike—have crushes from the time they go off to preschool. But as you reach puberty, those crushes may get bigger.

brave new world

Tiny crushes, which in first grade took up a corner of your brain, can become **huge, humongous, gigantic** crushes that make you look out the window for hours instead of studying for your math test.

Lots of crushes are daydreams. You might have a crush on a pop star. You might have a crush on a teacher or your older sibling's friend. You might have a crush on a kid at school who doesn't even know your name. These kinds of crushes can make you feel **wonderful** because . . .

you have **excited,** happy feelings,

you have fun **imaginings,**

you can feel romantic about someone **without the risk** that that person might hurt your feelings **(it's safe),**

and you will never have to face the fact that your crush is **not perfect.**

Crushes are also useful. A crush lets you try on new feelings, sort of like trying on clothes in a store. You can learn a lot without buying anything. You consider what you like in other people. You learn how to deal with frustration when you can't get what you want. It's all part of growing up.

Of course, you also might develop a crush on someone you actually know. Kids around you may be getting crushes, too. Some might even be speaking up and saying so. This can make life at school **very** different.

a typical day

Suddenly kids are talking about who likes who. School is a more gossipy, less private place. There's more intrigue—and more nervousness, too.

8:45 a.m. Sophia tells Addison she likes Ryan.

10:05 a.m. Addison tells Ryan that Sophia likes him. Ryan says, "Uh, well, Sophia's OK."

10:36 a.m. Maria writes her favorite movie star's name on her notebook cover for the 348th time.

11:05 a.m. Addison sends a text to ten of her closest friends (including Sophia) announcing that Sophia and Ryan are now together.

11:47 a.m. Taylor sits near Destiny at lunch. That's new. What does it mean? Destiny has no idea.

11:50 a.m. Sophia says hi to Ryan in the cafeteria. Ryan says hi back. They both sit with their friends.

12:01 p.m. Max and Gabriella ignore each other when they dump their trays. They are neighbors and good friends, but they never let on at school because they'd be teased.

1:30–1:45 p.m.

Sophia writes a note to Ryan and folds it up till it's the size of a wad of chewing gum. She gives it to Addison to deliver.

2:10 p.m.

Kayla and Jing and Autumn have a good time in gym teasing David and DeShay and Reese.

3:00–3:30 p.m.

Addison gives Sophia's note to Ryan. She thinks he looks cute when he's embarrassed. On the bus, Addison makes a list of all the kids she's liked this year. It looks like this:

1. Ryan (2 weeks)
2. Tyler (1 week)
3. Khalid (2 days)
4. David (3½ hours)
5. Maggie's brother Jonathan (in her dreams)

There were others first semester, but she lost count. She thinks maybe she'd like to go with Ryan again after he and Sophia break up. She figures her friend and her new crush will last about **two weeks.** Maybe **one.**

hormones

What is causing all this drama? For one thing, hormones.

Hormones are chemicals in the body. During puberty, a girl's hormones help her body develop into a woman's body, and a boy's hormones help his body develop into a man's body. In general, this happens a little sooner for girls. That's why girls are sometimes taller and physically more mature than boys up until high school.

Hormones cause lots of **emotional changes,** too. Your moods get stronger at the same time your body's growing in new, confusing ways. Throw in all the other things kids are often dealing with at this age—acne, body odor, braces. Small wonder if a girl finds romantic feelings hard to handle.

- Eye contact is normal.
- Thinking is normal.
- Talking is no big deal.

- Eye contact is iffy.
- No clue what to say.
- Heart is jumpy.
- Stomach is woozy.
- Thinking? Ha!

staying normal

I don't have any problem being myself around girls, but sometimes when boys are around, I can't seem to be me. I just act weird.
Breena

A lot of girls find it hard to act normal. The simplest thing—like passing an assignment to the kid in the next desk—may send clouds of questions rolling through your mind.

You start acting, **well, weird.** But there are ways you can control that.

galloping giggles

Jesse cracks a joke. You go heeheeheeheeheeheeheeheehee heeheeheeheeheeheeheeheeheeheeheeheeheeheeheehee heeheeheeheeheeheeheeheeheeheeheeheeheehee—and can't stop until the teacher walks up and raps on your desk.

A good joke deserves a good giggle. Lots of us may laugh when we're nervous, too, whether something's funny or not. That's OK up to a point, but you don't want to be the kid who giggles all the time. It makes you seem silly. And you're just not good company when you're out of control. So when the giggles attack, close your mouth, freeze your chest, and hold your breath for a moment. Glance away. Do something with your hands—grab a pencil, fool with the straps of your backpack. Concentrate on pulling yourself together, and don't let go till you do.

being fake

Nicholas is cute, Nathan is awesome, and Neo is cool. You have to walk past them all on the way to your locker. You put your chin in the air, pretend you're Miss Popularity, and hope they buy the act.

Most of us put up a front when we're nervous. It helps us hide our fears. But the goal is to relax and be yourself, not to pass yourself off as Miss Popularity. So don't overdo the cool. Release that chin. Picture yourself the way you are coming off the field after a winning game, singing along to your favorite song, or talking to your little sister. Picture you being you.

chatterbox

Angel is standing next to you in line. Suddenly you hear yourself jabbering away as if your mouth weren't connected to your brain.

Slow down. It will give you time to think before you speak. Don't run your words together. Take a breath between sentences. Ask questions. Conversations involve both people talking, after all. While Angel's responding, really listen. That will help you decide what to say next.

"liking" someone

I have a group of really great friends who are each unique and creative in their own way. Some of them happen to be boys. There's this one kid I've known since the third grade, but now that we're getting older, I'm starting to like him differently (if you know what I mean).
Meg

You've always had certain feelings about the people around you. You liked some a little, others a lot. That's still true, only now **romantic feelings** come and go by the day. Is that kid you have fun talking to a "friend" or something else? All of a sudden, you might not be quite sure. Answers to some basic questions would be nice.

a few basics

Q. Boys and girls are the same, but they're different, too. What gives?

A. Every person is an individual. Any boy, any girl, can be anything and do anything that's humanly possible. People are amazingly varied. When it comes to the person in front of you, there's no way to say, "He's this, she's that."

But it's also true that, as a group, boys are different from girls in certain ways. Some of those differences are physical. For instance, scientists have shown that girls' brains and boys' brains are different, physically and chemically. And boys typically have different hormones, which make for different emotions. Other differences are learned. From the time they're babies, boys and girls may get different messages about who they should be. Those messages vary widely depending on their families, where they live, and the times they're growing up in. But what's always true is that people's surroundings help shape who they are. So are boys and girls both the same and different? Yes.

Q. Stereotypes are a problem. "Girls like to wear pink" is a stereotype. But you do like pink. What should you do?

A. If you like pink, by all means wear pink. There's nothing in the world wrong with that. What's important is that the boy in the next desk can wear pink, too, if he wants to. A kid should get to pick what he or she likes best. That goes with clothes, hair, games, foods, books—whatever. We're all unique. Kids shouldn't feel stuck with choices they don't like because that's what boys and girls are "supposed" to be or do.

Q. Do all girls like boys?

A. No. Some girls get crushes on other girls. Some get crushes on both boys and girls. Others don't get crushes at all. The same variety exists with boys. It's all normal.

Q. Do you have to announce whether you're straight or gay or whatever, like on a sign-up sheet?

A. No. The point is not to find the right label. The point is to understand what makes you happy. So just pay attention to your feelings and form the relationships that seem right for you. If the day comes when you want to embrace a word for that, you can do so then.

Q. Does everybody agree on stereotypes, the differences between girls and boys, and who can like who?

A. No. But we should all be able to agree that every person deserves respect. A lot of bad stuff happens when people look at one another and think, *They're different from me, they shouldn't be like that*. Being different isn't bad. It's what people *are*. That's why the Golden Rule remains gold. Treat others the way you want to be treated yourself.

Q. How can you get someone to like you? You're thinking you need a makeover.

A. Attraction is a bit mysterious. Looks count, but not as much as you might think. Ask a bunch of kids what they look for in another person, and you'll hear:

a good personality

someone attractive, nice, and with a good sense of humor

smart, cute, fun to be around

someone who likes me for me

girls who are themselves—who aren't all phony and stuff

So go ahead and experiment with your looks. But before you buy a bucket of makeup or drop old friends for new ones to impress that special some-one, ask yourself, "Is this going to make me happier to be me?" If the answer is no, don't do it. The most attractive things about a person have to do with character—basics such as kindness, humor, and honesty. Set your sights on that, and the rest will take care of itself.

smart girl's GUIDE
American Girl
GETTING IT TOGETHER
how to organize your space, your stuff, your time—and your life

falling apart?

a disorganized day

Have you ever had a day like this?

7:07 a.m.
You wake up late—again. The bus is coming in 20 minutes, and you still have homework to do!

7:27 a.m.
The bus comes . . . and goes. Where are you? In your closet, searching for a shoe.

7:52 a.m.
Mom (who's mad) drops you off at school. You whip open your locker and get buried in an avalanche of papers.

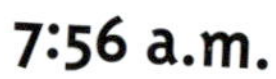

7:56 a.m.
You're late to math. At least you finished your homework. But wait! It's still at home on the kitchen counter!

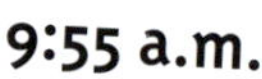

9:55 a.m.
Your stomach is growling. Too bad you didn't have time for breakfast.

11:17 a.m.
Time for gym. Where are your gym shoes? Oops! You forgot those, too.

1:45 p.m.
Ugh. Science test! How were you supposed to study on top of your other homework?

3:32 p.m.
Whew! You're finally home. You'll do homework right away—after a snack. And some time online.

4:55 p.m.
Dad's here to take you to dance practice! Already??? You race to your room to get changed.

7:20 p.m.
How can you do homework while your sister is watching your favorite movie? Hey, here's an idea! You'll get up early tomorrow and do homework then.

9:21 p.m.
As you drift off to sleep, you remember the bake sale. Tomorrow. You're supposed to bring a dozen cupcakes . . .

Yikes! What a day!

Was it bad luck?
No.
Are you a bad student?
No.
Lazy?
Nope.
Try **disorganized.**

When you're disorganized, your space gets cluttered and you can't find what you need. You're late. You forget things. You're always stressed out and frustrated—and your parents and teachers (and friends and siblings and pets . . .) might be getting frustrated with you, too.

Here's the good news: You can teach yourself tricks for staying on top of your stuff and your schedule. And when you start, you'll have more *yay!* days than *yikes!* days. You'll feel more relaxed. You'll laugh more and worry less. You'll be taking charge of your life—and that's one of the best feelings of all.

Quiz

what trips you up?

Maybe you keep a tidy room but can't keep track of time. Maybe you hate being late, but you don't mind dust bunnies—and books and sweaters and papers and markers and hair clips and socks—stuffed under your bed. Which of these sound like you?

I finished my homework—honest! I just can't remember where I put it.

Mornings are so hectic! I'm already stressed out by the time I get to school.

I'd make my bed, except then I'd have to find someplace to put my clothes. And my stuffed animals. And my books.

Sometimes I'm surprised by tests at school. How come no one else seems to be?

Are those clothes on the floor clean or dirty? It's hard to tell.

I keep my alarm clock by my bed so I can hit "snooze" in my sleep.

My backpack might weigh more than I do. I'm not exactly sure what's in there.

My reasons for not doing homework are more creative than my actual work.

Okay, I admit it. I once found moldy food in my backpack. Okay, twice . . .

I've gotten a bad grade because of a missed assignment or two . . . or three.

I forget my lunch, homework, or sports stuff at least once a week. Thank goodness my parents are just a phone call away.

Put things off till the last minute? Who, me?

Do homework in my bedroom? No way. My brain shuts down with all the clutter in there.

I totally forgot about my science project. Mom and I stayed up late to get it done, but I think the glue's still wet.

I finally found my missing book report! Crumpled up at the bottom of my backpack. At the end of the school year. *Sigh.*

I need a personal secretary to manage my busy schedule.

A girl could trip and sprain her ankle walking across my room.

Who needs a calendar? My parents keep track of my schedule for me.

There's at least one drawer in my room that's too full to close.

Running late is one of my best forms of exercise.

Answers

If you chose **mostly blue,** your stuff is tripping you up! But you can cut the clutter and take control of your space. Read the "At School" section of this book for tips on cleaning out your backpack and giving your locker a makeover. Then read on for fun ways to redo your room so that you can find what you need, when you need it—and love being there.

If you chose **mostly purple,** it's time to get in touch with time. Read the "About Time" section for ways to make friends with clocks and calendars. Practice tracking time while you're getting ready in the morning or doing homework at night. Once you figure out where your time is going, you can save it for the things that matter most to you.

If you chose **both colors,** you're like many girls (and a lot of adults). But not to worry. You can get it together, one step at a time. Read the "One Small Step" ideas in every section for quick, easy ways to cut clutter and take charge of your schedule. Those small steps will give you the confidence to make bigger changes later on.

7 reasons to get it together

Sure, getting organized takes a little time and work. But it's worth it! Here's why.

1. You'll save yourself loads of time later on—time you used to spend searching for things under your bed or at the bottom of your backpack.

2. You'll feel good being in your room, and you'll be proud to show it off to friends.

3. You'll argue less with your parents about things like getting homework done and being on time.

4. Instead of waking up in a panic, you'll wake up feeling calm and peaceful.

5. Your teachers will notice that something's up with you. You might even get better grades!

6. You'll have more time for the things you really want to do.

7. You'll feel in control of your life and ready to tackle **ANYTHING!**

we did it!

Here are some ways that girls like you have found to manage their stuff, their space, and their schedule.

Every time my school binder gets full, I clean it out. I look at every paper and ask, "Do I NEED this for my learning?" If not, I recycle it. My binder is much lighter now.
—Nina

I put labels on all my drawers so I always have specific places to put everything. My room is so much cleaner and more organized!
—Bethany

I write everything I need to do on a sticky note. It's a friendly little list.
—Chloe

I used to be in a rush in the morning. Then I found out it works really well to lay out my clothes, put my homework in my backpack, and make my lunch the night before. When I get up, I'm all ready to go.
—Makenna

Because I forget EVERYTHING, I write a to-do list in a small notebook that I carry around, even at school. This makes me feel amazing! I know I can relax without worrying I forgot something.

—Maddy

I started setting my alarm clock 10 minutes earlier, and it made my mornings go sooo much smoother.

—Gracie

I use a big whiteboard for my schedule, homework, and any other info I need to know. It makes me feel like I have all my thoughts together.

—Caitlyn

I do my homework as soon as possible because it makes my evenings more calm and relaxed.

—Flo

I organized my whole room lately, and that made me feel REALLY fantastic!!!

—Abby

You're getting older. You're going new places and doing new things. You have more independence—and more responsibility, too. Suddenly everybody expects you to act more like an adult and less like a little kid. But that's not always easy to do. Manners can help.

let's talk

me first?

There's a voice inside each of us that says

"Me first."

It tells us to please ourselves—to take what we want and do what we like, never mind about anybody else. If "me first" had its way, we'd spend our days trampling on one another's rights and feelings, and pretty soon the world would be a snarling mess.

This is where manners come in.

Manners aren't a bunch of rules dreamed up by fusspots who want to cramp your style. Manners help people get along together. They make us nicer. They teach us to put ourselves in the other person's shoes.

A girl who chooses to use good manners is telling the world she believes that other people matter as much as she does. She's saying that life isn't about what one person does for herself but about what people can do together for the common good.

So who decides what's polite and what's not? We all do.

When we talk about manners, we're talking about how most people in a certain time and place think people should behave. What's polite in one country isn't always polite in another. What was rude fifty years ago isn't always rude today. Manners depend a lot on custom—and different customs often live side by side.

In a way, manners are not so much a set of rules as they are a language you use to tell other people what they can expect from you. The better you know the language, the more you can say.

Are you trustworthy?

Do you think only of yourself?

Would you make a good friend or a poor one?

after you

The way you talk with a good friend when you're flopped on the grass is very different from the way you talk to the principal in the hallway at school. You change your style without thinking. And that's good.

Manners recognize differences between people. There are certain things people do that say "You're number one" or "Your needs come first." These actions are called *signs of deference*, and to lots of people they symbolize good manners. They're rooted in tradition—and in kindness. Deference turns up in all sorts of ways in manners, but here are a few of the big ones.

Hold doors open for adults. When you and a friend are going through a doorway, let her go ahead of you.

Guests go first. When you're pouring lemonade, pour your friend's glass before you pour your own. When you start a game, let her have the first turn. And when there's only one cookie left? You know who gets it.

Give up your seat on a crowded bus or subway to anybody who looks as if they need to sit down more than you do. This includes older people and people with babies or small children.

Men and women have followed different rules in the past. For many years, men were expected to give all these same signs of deference to women. A polite man opened doors for a woman and let her enter first. He stood when a woman entered a room at a party and offered her his seat. He walked between a woman and the curb on city streets to protect her from any rain or dirt kicked up by a passing car. Many people keep up these traditions today. Others prefer to see women show their strength and independence by doing these things for themselves.

good impressions

We all know we shouldn't judge a book by its cover, but the fact is that most of us do make judgments about others based on how they look and talk. This is especially true if we're meeting someone for the first time.

Don't let this business of appearances spook you. Instead, try out the tips on these pages. You'll *look* more confident, and that can often make you *feel* more confident. The more you practice these things, the more natural they'll seem. A little work on the outside girl lets the girl inside shine through—and that, of course, is the entire point.

Stand tall

Your body says a lot about what you think of yourself. Hold your head up. Pull your shoulders back. Talk in a strong voice. Walk like a girl who's ready to meet the world, and you'll begin to feel like one. You'll find that others will see you that way, too.

Make eye contact

Look people in the eye. It shows that you're friendly and honest. It also tells others that you're interested in them and in what they're saying.

Say hello

"Hi" means "I know you. I'm glad to see you, even if we're not going to stop and talk." Silence means . . . well, who knows? It might mean "I'm mad at you" or "I don't like you"—or simply "There you are, but so what?"

Use names

Greet people by name. It shows that you care who they are, which makes them feel good.

If you have trouble remembering names, practice saying them when they're fresh in your mind. For instance, if you're introduced to a new girl, say her name right away. (If you didn't quite catch it, ask her to repeat it until you do.) Then use her name several more times before the conversation's done. The more often you use the name today, the better chance you have of remembering it tomorrow.

Shake hands

Step up and shake hands when you're saying hello to an adult, especially if the situation is fairly formal. Offer your right hand (even if you're left-handed) and say the person's name: "Hi, Ms. Puptent." When she puts her hand in yours, clasp it firmly for one quick shake.

choose your words

Manners are all about communication, so put some thought into the words you use to express yourself.

Those **magic words** people have been telling you about all your life really are sort of magic. Say "please" and people cooperate. Say "thank you" and get a smile. These words make everything a little easier and happier—both for others and for you.

Other words sneak into conversations without you even realizing you're saying them. **Junk words,** for instance. Words that have nothing to do with the sense of a sentence can be, you know, like, so annoying, like, if you, like, use them constantly, you know?

There are also **lazy words—**hmm, nah, eh, huh, yeah. We all use them, but overdo it and you'll give the impression that you dragged yourself out of a deep sleep to have this conversation and wish you were still in bed.

Lots of kids use **put-downs** when they're kidding around with their friends. "So what?" "Who cares?" "Shut up." Put-downs are supposed to be funny. Maybe. But a put-down always makes another person feel a bit dumber than she did before you said it. Put-downs sting—maybe a little, maybe a lot.

Keep in mind that **words that work with one kind of person might not work with another.** For instance, you and a close friend may say "duh" just in fun. But if you use "duh" with a kid you don't know well, it's hurtful. And if you use it with an adult, it's insulting.

Swear words: You don't need them. With hundreds of thousands of words to choose from, why use the ones that were designed to insult and offend people?

Finally, pleasant words don't count if the **tone of your voice** says something entirely different. Yell "I'm sorry," and it means you're not.

respect

It all boils down to respect.

Your manners tell other people that you respect them. Your manners also say that you respect yourself.

You're strong and self-reliant—you don't have to put yourself first. You're in control. You're poised. You know that offering respect to people who are older than you are and people in authority doesn't take away from the respect you have for yourself.

In fact, you know that **the more respect you give, the more you get.**

In a world with a lot of selfishness, you choose kindness and honor.

Who wouldn't respect a person like that?

table manners

People need more than good food to enjoy a meal. They also need good company. That's where table manners come in. Table manners remind us how to share and how to be considerate—not to mention how to avoid grossing other people out. They make mealtimes more pleasant at home and are one of the first things people will notice about you when you're a guest.

Help out

Stick your nose in the kitchen before dinner and ask the cook if there's anything you can do to help. Pour drinks, get out the butter, or set the table. A simple place setting looks like this, with the knife blade turned toward the plate.

Wait to begin

Come when you're called. Sit down and put your napkin in your lap, but don't start digging into the biscuits until everyone else is seated, too—including the cook. If you're a guest, tradition says to wait for the host to take a bite of food. Then you can begin as well.

Get in the spirit

Ditch the electronics. No phone calls, no texting, no computers, no tablets, no TV. Pay attention to the people sitting around you instead. Talk. Tell a story or two about your day. Ask a few questions. How did volleyball practice go for your brother? Did your mom see another coyote on her way to work? Has everybody heard about the Trojan horse the art teacher is building for Greek Week at school? See what kind of conversation you can get going.

Cutting your meat

Hold your knife and fork like this:

(Don't hold them in your fists.) **Cut one small piece at a time.** Transfer your fork back to your right hand (if you're right-handed) and set your knife on the plate as you eat.

Directing traffic

Food is passed to the right. If serving dishes are going both right and left, they're going to collide like cars on a one-way street. At posh parties and restaurants, waiters serve from the right and pick up used dishes from the left.

Helping yourself

Take the portion nearest you. Leave the utensils neatly together, handles out, so that the next person doesn't have to fish through the sauce to get to them. If it's a big dish, help the next person by holding it while he serves himself.

Second helpings

At home, once everybody has been served, it's OK to ask for second helpings. If you're a guest in someone else's home, however, you should hold off. If there's enough food for seconds, the hosts will offer it.

Reaching

If for some reason a dish didn't get to you, ask for it: "Please pass the rolls." If you reach across the table, your elbow may end up in your pa's peas.

Chewing

Squishy sounds + the sight of chewed-up food
=
disgusting.

That's why you should **chew with your mouth closed** and avoid talking while you're doing it.

At rest

If you've stopped eating for a minute, position your silverware like this:

At a restaurant or fancy dinner, this tells the server that you've paused but you're not finished.

Elbows

So why do you have to keep your elbows off the table, anyway? Because slouching over your plate makes you look lazy and bored.

Acting goofy

Blowing bubbles in your milk or making a castle of your mashed potatoes tells the cook you'd rather play with the food than eat it. Does the cook appreciate this? Nope.

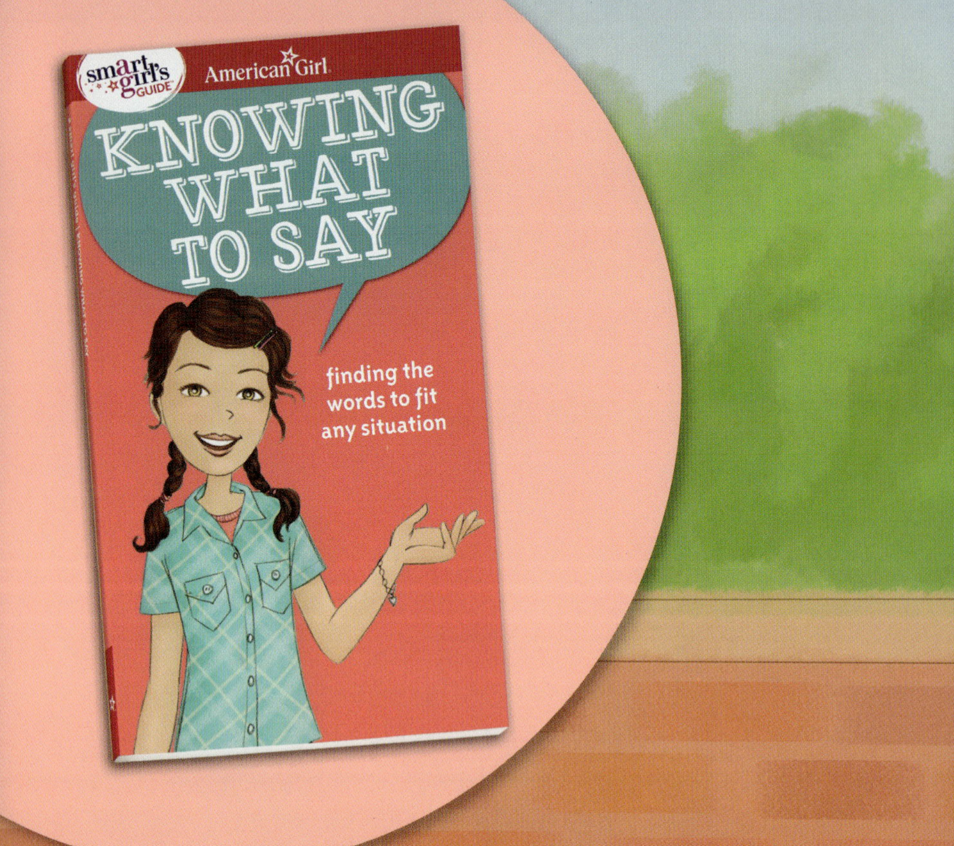

"We were just making small talk." This saying means the conversation was easy and light. With small talk, you're not sharing your deepest, darkest secrets, but it's still an important part of everyday conversation. Small talk says that I want to know you better, that I care about you, and that what you say matters.

small talk

25 things to say after "hi"

Imagine that you want to start a conversation with the girl waiting next to you at the city bus stop, but you don't know what to say. After saying hi, try one of these questions to get the talk going.

1. I'm (your name). What's your name? 2. How's it going? 3. What school do you go to? 4. I'm in fifth grade. What grade are you in? 5. Do you take this bus often? 6. Do you ever listen to podcasts? 7. Want to play a game while we wait? 8. Have you seen (the latest movie)? 9. I wish I had brought my book. Do you like to read? 10. Can you believe how (hot/rainy/cold) it is? 11. I thought I'd be late. Have you been here long? 12. So, what do you like to do when you're not waiting for buses? 13. Tonight (a TV show) is on. Do you ever watch that? 14. Would you like a piece of gum? 15. I have a ton of homework. Does your teacher assign a lot of work? 16. I love your (something she's wearing). Is it your favorite color? 17. Do you know what time it is? 18. I can't wait for the weekend. I'm (give a detail about your plans). How about you? 19. I'm excited to get home to my new puppy. Do you have pets? 20. Have you lived here long? 21. I love your hair. Did you braid it yourself? 22. Want to sit together? 23. Do you think the bus will be late today? 24. Do you ride the school bus, too? 25. Where are you going today?

25 questions to know someone better

Now imagine that you've talked to this girl a few times before, and you think you have a lot in common. Try these questions to get to know her even better.

1. When is your birthday? 2. Have you ever tried out for a sport? 3. What's your favorite candy? 4. Have you ever won anything? 5. Are you nervous about middle school? High school? 6. Do you like to cook? 7. Have you ever lived in a different state? Country? 8. Who is your favorite teacher? Why? 9. Do you collect anything? 10. What's your biggest fear? 11. Do you know what you want to be next Halloween? 12. Do you have any vacations coming up? 13. Where's your favorite place to hang out with your friends? 14. How many people are in your family? 15. Do you have a favorite singer? 16. Have you ever gotten lost? What did you do? 17. Do you have your own computer at home? 18. What's your favorite thing to do? 19. Do you have your own room? 20. What's your favorite show? 21. Do you have a dream job? 22. Do you like to ride on roller coasters? 23. Do you ever write poems or stories? 24. What kind of books do you like to read? 25. If you could live anywhere, where would it be?

what to say

when you're the new girl

Starting a conversation takes courage. But here's the thing—it only takes one sentence to get the talk going. So start with your name and an easy question. Then see where things go. It looks like this:

If you're new in school and want to meet girls at lunch:

I'm Angela. How's it going? OK if I sit here?

If you just arrive at camp and walk in the cabin to find three sets of eyes staring at you:

Hi! I'm Christina. So are the bunks first come, first served?

If your teacher puts you on a committee to choose library books:

Hi, guys! I'm Olivia. I love to read, so this should be a lot of fun.

If you join a club, and you're asked to tell everyone a little about yourself:

I'm Samantha, I'm 11, I have one sister, and I play the violin.

Take it slow. Never share private information until you know the person better.

Share your point of view

Sharing your thoughts, feelings, and opinions about things will help your friendship grow. By giving your point of view, you're letting others get to know you, and by speaking up, you're allowing your confidence to shine.

BIG IMPORTANT POINT

Part one of being confident is having a point of view. But part two is *really* caring about what others think. So after you've shared, invite others to share, too.

what to say

when someone else is new

Take the time to talk with someone new. If you've ever been "the new girl," you know how much it matters. So when you get the chance to brighten someone's day—take it.

If you want to meet a new girl, and she looks really shy:

Hi, I'm Bethany. Are you finding everything OK?

If you want to meet the new girl on the soccer team, but you're not sure what to say to her:

Hi, I'm Leigh. What position do you like to play?

If you want to invite the new girl to get together outside of school for the first time:

Do you want to go with me to the school carnival this weekend? It's always fun.

If you want to welcome a new girl to your scouting troop:

Hi, I'm Kasia. Today we're making raffia flowers. Would you like to sit with Ella and me?

If the new girl in class is assigned as your science partner:

Nice to meet you, Alex. Have you ever had to make invisible ink before?

Chitchatting Clues

Having a tough time getting the conversation started? Try this: Look around you and find a person, place, or thing to talk about. Now, strike up a conversation. Check out these examples.

what to say

when talking with adults

Adults don't have to be intimidating, but it's simple to make small talk if you really *listen* to what the adult is asking. Then add to the conversation with a bit more information or by asking a question.

If the uncle you haven't seen since you were a little kid asks, "What have you been doing for fun lately?"

Instead of this: "Not much."

Say this: I joined a travel soccer team—that's been fun. Mom said you went to Spain. What was that like?

If your great-aunt says, "Look how much you've grown!"

Instead of this: "I guess."

Say this: Yeah, I've grown out of my clothes this year. The doctor says I'm going to be taller than Mom.

If your friend's dad asks, "So what are you two hard at work on?"

Instead of this: "Homework."

Say this: Carly and I have to do homework about Mexico, so we're looking for pictures in these old travel magazines.

If you're waiting for class to start and your art teacher asks, "Are you ready to make clay flowers today?"

Instead of this: "OK."

Say this: I'm excited. My mom has a flower garden, so I already have ideas that I want to try.

If a woman in your mother's book club sees you and asks, "Gabriella, do you like to read?"

Instead of this: "Uh-huh."

Say this: I read all kinds of books, but I love graphic novels. Have you ever read one of those?

If your neighbor is working in her garden and asks, "What have your parents been up to lately?"

Instead of this: "I don't know."

Say this: Mom's busy with work, and Dad's cleaning out the garage.

A TIP

When someone asks you a question, it's important that you say something other than "good" or "nothing." If you don't have much to say, ask a question. Questions help move the conversation back and forth like a ball in a tennis match—only in the end, you're both winners.

compliments

Admiring something about a person is a great way to start a conversation. It opens the door to even more talking and sharing. And who doesn't love a compliment? Check out these dos and don'ts when giving and receiving compliments.

GIVING compliments

- Do speak from the heart with honest and positive comments.
  Instead of this: "I liked your speech."

Say this: Your speech really kept my attention. You're a great speaker.

- Do give specific details about what you like or liked.
  Instead of this: "Cool poem."

Say this: I loved your haiku, especially the line about your cat being a sushi specialist.

- Don't expect a compliment back.
  Instead of this: "Nice sweater. Do you like mine?"

Say this: You look pretty in that sweater. It makes your eyes look so blue.

- Don't add a "but" statement after complimenting someone.
  Instead of this: "Your party was fun, BUT my sister's party was amazing."

Say this: Your party rocked! I loved your decorations.

RECEIVING compliments

- Do accept compliments with a sincere thank-you.
  Compliment: "Your artwork is really cool."
  Instead of this: "Yeah, a lot of people have given me compliments."

  Say this: Thank you! That means a lot to me.

- Do give credit to a partner or partners if you receive a compliment on a group project.
  Compliment: "What a great project on recycling!"
  Instead of this: "Thanks!"

  Say this: Thanks! I did the presentation, but Sophie and Natalie did most of the writing.

- Don't agree in a bragging way.
  Compliment: "Another 100! You're so smart."
  Instead of this: "Yeah, I think it's easy to get all A's."

  Say this: Thanks. I really like social studies.

- Don't disagree or cut yourself down when receiving a compliment.
  Compliment: "Wow! You have an awesome voice."
  Instead of this: "Thanks, but I don't think I sang that well."

smart girl's GUIDE
American Girl
RACE & INCLUSION
standing up to racism and building a better world

Becoming anti-
racist starts by
looking inward

getting started

By practicing anti-racism, you work to make lives better for all people. But that's a big challenge! The idea of improving schools for Mexican Americans or getting better jobs for Indigenous peoples feels overwhelming and impossible to accomplish. You might think, "I'm just one person. How can I help?" Start small by noticing what you *can* do.

NEIGHBORS

friends

School

family

BOOK CLUB

My mini-worlds

Imagine your world as a collection of bubbles—these are the miniature societies you're a part of. Your family is your closest bubble. Other bubbles include your friends, your neighbors, your school, and other groups you belong to. Even if you feel as though you don't have power to create big change in the world, there are smaller bubbles where you do have influence.

Once you've identified who is in your bubbles, you can pinpoint ways to share your opinions and knowledge with others. A dinner conversation can help your younger brother understand anti-racism. Or asking your book club to read a book by a Black author whose main character is different from the main characters in other books you've read can encourage your friends to see more perspectives. The idea is to expand the thinking within your mini-worlds to include new and different points of view.

living inside a bubble

Thinking about our bubbles is helpful because they show who's closest to us, but they can also cause problems. We often don't see what life is like outside our bubbles.

What shapes your world?

Most white people live in mostly white neighborhoods, go to mostly white schools, and hang out with other white people. They generally read books and watch movies and TV shows about white people. It becomes easy for white people to assume everyone lives like them—or *should* live like them. Why? Because they are living inside their bubble. But think about what it's like for people who live outside that bubble.

What's going on outside?

How might it feel if you . . .

- didn't have books, shows, or movies with characters who looked like you?
- didn't have school lessons about people who looked like you?
- went to a school with a dress code that didn't allow you to wear your hair the way it grows out of your head?
- were the only member of your racial group in most places?
- learned more than one language and then people made fun of you for having an accent?

The problem with bubbles

When we are inside our bubbles, we feel safe and comfortable, and we start to believe our way of living is the right way—or the only way. Inside your bubble, you might forget that not everyone lives like you. Those outside your bubble may dress differently, act differently, or talk differently, but that doesn't mean that their lives are bad, wrong, or less worthy. And too often, those on the outside are made to feel more stupid, ugly, and bad than those inside. If you stay inside your bubble and don't recognize that differences are good, you're going to miss out on a lot of great experiences!

outside your bubble

People who aren't in your bubble probably live a different life than you do. For example, Madison and Lucy might assume that Selah's life is the same as theirs because they all go to the same school, enjoy Drama Club, have similar family structures, and share the same hopes and worries about their future. But Lucy and Madison don't realize how different life is for Selah. She has other issues, such as people constantly wanting to touch her hair or never getting lead roles in Drama Club productions because people believe that some roles can only be played by white people.

Living in your bubble makes it feel like your way of doing things is the only way to do things. If you have access to good food, clothing, jobs, education, housing, and safety, it might be hard to realize how hard life is for people who don't. Worst of all, your bubble will give you all kinds of reasons to think others shouldn't have these things.

Think about your bubble and answer these questions:

What is life like for others or people who are different from me?

How do I feel about those people?

What am I missing out on by only living inside my bubble?

Maybe you've never had to think about people outside your bubble before, so you might have trouble answering these questions. Read on to learn some skills for getting outside your bubble.

beyond your bubble

To venture outside your bubble, start by thinking about what you want to learn. Ask yourself, What do I want to know? How do I want to grow?

If you were trying to learn something new in history class, what would you do? You'd probably think about where you could get that information—whether by reading, researching, or talking to other people. To learn about the experiences of others, you can do the same thing. Make a learning plan by pinpointing what you want to learn, how you're going to learn it, and how you'll share what you've learned with others.

Mini-challenges

How many of these can you do to expand your bubble?

- ☐ With a parent or teacher, find five videos that help you learn about others' life experiences and points of view.
- ☐ Ask a librarian to help you look up articles about anti-racism or discover three books by authors of color whose main characters live in bubbles unlike yours.
- ☐ Learn another language, even if it's just some basic vocabulary or a few phrases.
- ☐ Watch a show or movie featuring people from a different racial group.
- ☐ Listen to a different kind of music than you usually do.
- ☐ Research your community to learn about the racial minorities in your city. Are there cultural events put on by those groups you could attend?
- ☐ Find recipes to make food you've never tried before. Or seek out a new restaurant for your family's next night out!
- ☐ Spin a globe and place your finger on a random spot. Research that country's people, food, music, art, history, politics, and culture.

Be Anti-RACIST

Learn

Try something new

Get Ideas

Go beyond your bubble

Going beyond your bubble can be fun! But be careful: If you're a white girl, spending an afternoon watching a movie about a Black girl doesn't mean you understand her life, her story, or the experiences of other Black people. Anti-racism is a lifelong process! Madison can try to understand what life is like for Selah, but she will never fully get it. It's still important to keep trying to better understand other people and their experiences.

looking through your lens

If you wear glasses, you know that you see things differently when you take your glasses off. In the same way, your bubble can be like a lens that influences how you see the world.

Seeing what's real

Some lenses make white people look good, hardworking, trustworthy, and kind but make people of color look bad, lazy, mean, and dangerous. Even people who want to fight racism have biased thoughts and see people of color with fear, suspicion, or distrust. Why? One reason is because the lens we use to look at people outside our bubbles causes us to see stereotypes of people instead of who they really are.

Sometimes stereotypes lump all people from the same race together and create assumptions about an entire group of people. An example of a stereotype is that *all* Black people are great athletes or that *all* Asian Americans are math whizzes. It might be true that some people in a group align with a stereotype, but no stereotype is true for all the people in a group. Big statements like that aren't true about *any* group! But when we never encounter people outside our own bubbles, we might believe those false stereotypes.

What are some stereotypes that you are aware of? What are some stereotypes about the group *you* belong to?

Has anyone made assumptions about you based on your age? At some point in your life, you've probably had to explain to an adult that you are capable of doing something basic—like making your own breakfast—when they assumed you couldn't handle that task. Looking at you through that lens—that is, a stereotype based on your age—an adult made an assumption about you that isn't true. How does it make you feel when someone assumes just because you're a kid, you can't handle independence and responsibility?

This is how people of color can feel much of the time. Imagine how Selah feels in a club, school, and society where people assume negative things about her just because of the color of her skin.

Quiz

are you ready for new lenses?

Check the statements that might be true about you.

- ★ I like that Wednesday mornings are "Waffle Wednesdays" no matter what!
- ♥ I love to rearrange the furniture in my room—it always feels like a brand-new space even with the same stuff.
- ★ My friends know that when they come over for my birthday, they'll always get double chocolate cupcakes with lots of rainbow sprinkles!
- ♥ When I get my hair cut, you can count on me trying something new. I love a fresh look!
- ★ I've read my favorite book so many times I can't count. It always makes me feel good.
- ♥ When my dad surprises us with one of his new recipes, I'm excited. He's a great cook!
- ★ Going to the same camp every summer is my favorite week of the year.
- ♥ If there's an after-school club I want to join, I'll try it even if my friends aren't interested. Why not?
- ★ I've played goalie on my soccer team since I can remember.
- ♥ I think it would be so fun if my family went on a vacation, but our parents didn't tell us where we were going first.

If you chose mostly stars, you know what you like! Consider exploring new experiences or ideas, even if it means not eating waffles on Wednesdays. When you start to mix it up, you'll discover new foods, books, and activities that will light up your life. Go for it—you have nothing to lose!

If you chose mostly hearts, you're ready for a new challenge—and a new way to view the world! You'll never say no to a different way of thinking or a new experience. Use your enthusiasm to get others excited about learning and trying out different foods, cultural celebrations, books, and movies.

Flip the script

How you think and talk about differences is a big deal. Just because something isn't what you like or grew up doing doesn't mean it's wrong or bad. By being curious and learning more, you can change your thinking to celebrate differences.

When you encounter something new, how do you react? Do you turn your nose up at new foods or stare at people who are wearing clothing that's different from yours? Use these ideas to change your mindset.

Instead of saying (or thinking):	Flip the script! Try:
That head covering looks dumb.	Your headscarf is so pretty. Can you tell me what it's called so I use the right word?
Ew! What's in your lunch?	I've never seen rice like that. What's in it?
Your parents don't speak English?!	That's cool you know another language!
I would never eat that.	Can I try some? I've never tasted that.
That sounds like a weird way to celebrate a holiday.	How fun! I've never thought of that.

If you're interested in learning more about different cultural traditions, visit your school or public library and ask the librarian for help.

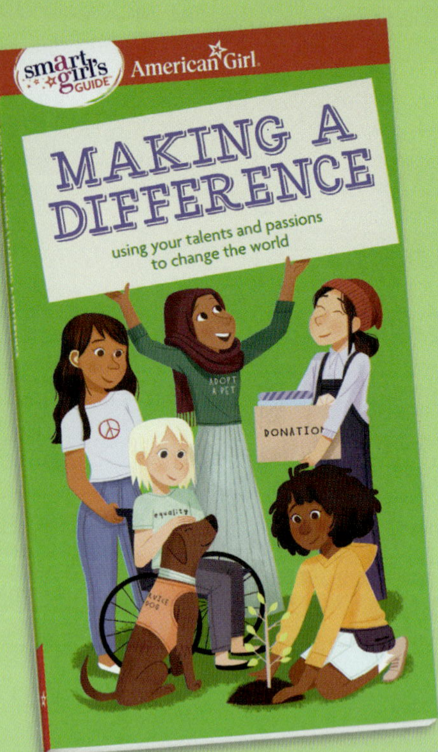

What happens when you drop a pebble into a calm pond? The ripples from the stone go far beyond the spot where the pebble sank. They travel out in rings that expand across the pond's surface. Think of your actions and words as the pebble. One small action can cause ripples bigger than you ever dreamed, and your actions can help change the world.

the ripple effect

be the change

So, you want to make a difference? Great! Everything you need to change the world is already inside you.

Maybe you feel a little flicker of joy inside when you help others.
No matter the reason, you want to make the world a better place. Let's get to work!

check it out

Why do you want to change the world? What does that pebble mean to you? Put a check next to each statement that feels right. Knowing why you want to make a difference can help you figure out what causes to dedicate your time and energy to.

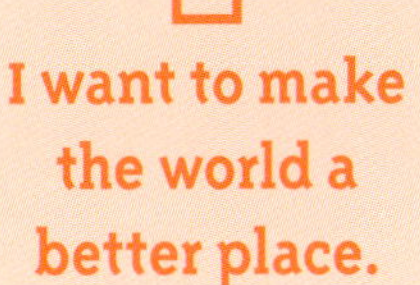

☐ I want to make the world a better place.

☐ I like teaching others.

☐ Helping gives me a sense of purpose.

☐ I want to learn more about my community and the world.

☐ I want my community to be safe for everyone.

All these reasons are worthwhile, and they might change as you grow. Do you have any other reasons for wanting to help? Jot them down in a notebook and keep it nearby. The statements you checked will help you decide what to focus on and how you'll make positive change in the world.

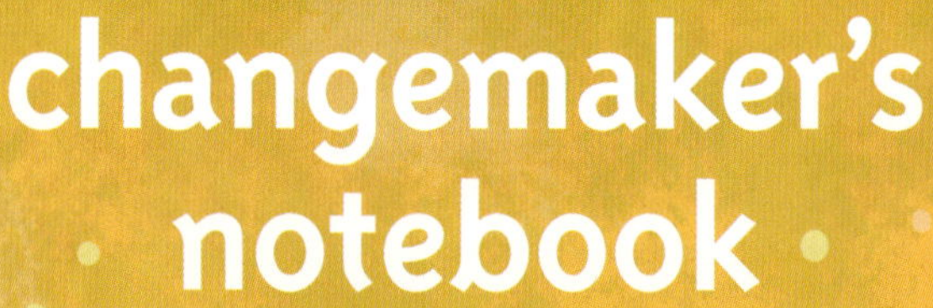

changemaker's notebook

It can be helpful to keep all your notes, ideas, and research in one place. Fill your changemaker's notebook with questions, concerns, and facts you learn about the issue you're researching. This is a great place to begin jotting down ideas or plans about how you'll take action.

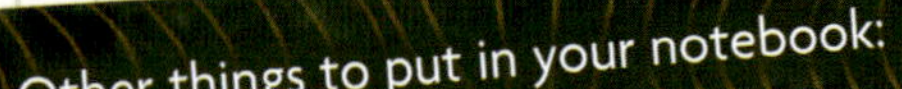

Other things to put in your notebook:

Clippings from magazines, articles, and posters

Inspirational sayings that motivate you

THERE IS NO PLANET B

Pictures of leaders you look up to
Sketches or doodles that relate to the cause you care about
Quotes from blogs or podcasts
"Mother Earth doesn't need us, but we need her."
– Autumn Peltier
Facts that relate to the cause
73: percent of beach litter that is plastic
450: number of years it takes for a plastic bottle to decompose
12: number of minutes a plastic bag is in use

what's activism?

Activism = bringing change to an issue or problem in the world, your community, or your life.

An activist = someone helping to change an issue that's important to them.

nowledge is POWER
Girls deserve the same rights as BOYS
Support Girls' Education
Educate GIRLS 4 success
EDUCATION FOR ALL
"Principal Hale, switching to reusable plates in the cafeteria would be awesome for the environment. Is this something we can talk about?"
Principal Hale

empathy, always

When things start to feel too big or too frustrating (and that can happen when you're an activist), take a deep breath and remember how important empathy is.

Having empathy means trying to understand someone else's feelings and having compassion for them. It's the ability to put yourself in someone else's shoes to understand their point of view and what they might be going through. Empathy is what connects us to one another and our world, and it's what inspires us to take action to try to ensure that everything and everyone is happy, healthy, and safe.

This big, beautiful world we live in is made up of an endless variety of people, creatures, environments, and habitats. We look different, act different, practice different religions, speak different languages, come from different cultures and countries, and have different perspectives. But empathy reminds us that we're all living on the same planet. And our differences make us unique and beautiful.

When you practice empathy and compassion for others, you are changing the world. You're more likely to be kind, patient, and loving with your words and actions if you truly value the planet and everything and everyone on it. By opening your heart and mind to diverse perspectives and experiences, you are sharpening your empathy skills and being the best activist you can be.

smart girl's GUIDE
American Girl
MONEY
how to make it, save it, and spend it
1¢
25¢
5¢
1¢
25¢
5¢
25¢
1¢
1¢
5¢
5¢

money!
money?

a girl and her money

Money. It's great to have, fun to spend, and (for some of us, anyway) hard to keep. As an example, think how much money has flowed through Alana's hands just this month…

There's her allowance,

the money she gets for lunch every day,

the money her parents gave her for the movies,

and the check her Aunt Maud sent for her birthday.

That's at least $100 in four short weeks!

Why, there could be $1,000 a year coming and going through Alana's wallet.

Who knew!

Yet if you stop and think about it, there is money flowing in and out of pockets all around you. Where does it all come from?

In a word:

work.

If you have a quarter in your pocket, it's because at some point someone earned it—maybe you, maybe your parents, maybe an aunt, maybe someone else. But *someone*.

your $ style

Which sounds more like you? Circle your answers.

1. "Where's that gift card you got for your birthday?" asks your mom. You say . . .

a. "In my dresser drawer. I'm still thinking about what I want."

b. "Beats me." (In fact, it's under your bed, along with a petrified licorice rope and some dust balls the size of Chicago.)

2. "That will be four dollars," says the saleswoman. You . . .

a. hand her the money.

b. say, "Uh—." You didn't check the prices. You have only $2.51.

3. You keep your money . . .

a. in the bank on your desk.

b. in piles all over your room. And at the bottom of your backpack. And in the pockets of the clothes you wore yesterday. There may be some on the floor of the car, too.

4. "How much did you spend at the game?" asks your dad. You . . .

a. tell him.

b. check your pockets. Everything, evidently.

5. You've done it again—left your gloves someplace. You . . .

a. check the lost-and-found and everyplace else you can think of.

b. borrow your brother's. You can always get new gloves.

6. "Here's your change," says the clerk. You . . .

a. put the bills neatly into your wallet.

b. toss bills and coins into the open mouth of your purse. Bombs away!

Answers

If you answered **mostly b's,** you're operating as if money and the things it buys have no value. But they do. Would you walk into a store and knowingly pay $5 for a $3 pen? Not likely. Yet if you go through the world blind to the value of what you've got, the results may be about the same. You're losing out.

If you answered **mostly a's,** you're not just tidy, you're knowledgeable. You know how much money you have. You know what you're spending. You know what's left. Keeping track gives you a better sense of what the money in your purse is really worth. When you see a snazzy barrette at the checkout, you'll know not only whether you have enough money to buy it but whether you really should.

a big truth

Money smarts begin with **good habits** and **just plain paying attention.**

money emotions

You've probably had all kinds of feelings about money.

You also have habits and attitudes that have been shaped by your family. A girl whose parents talk with ease about family finances will think differently about money than a girl whose parents worry or argue when the bills arrive. A girl who's grown up shopping the sales with her mom will likely have different spending habits than a girl who has only seen her mom buy freely. A girl's experiences may incline her to like or dislike people with more money—or to like or dislike people with less.

All this means that your feelings about money may be complicated. But the way you *use* money doesn't have to be.

When it comes to making decisions about money, keep your head cool and your thinking clear. Let three basic questions be your guide:

1. **Where are you now in terms of money?**

2. **Where do you want to go?**

3. **How do you get there?**

* greed
* anxiety
* pride
* happiness
* jealousy
* generosity

allowance

A lot of girls get their first experience managing money when they first get an allowance. Here's what some girls have to say about how it works in their homes:

"I get an allowance. My mom likes the fact that I am not bugging her for money. Having my own money has helped me learn how to manage money."

—Alex

"I only get an allowance when I do all my chores, like feeding the animals, putting my laundry away, and just picking up after myself. Chores are not my favorite pastime, but I do love my allowance!"

—Abigail

"I earn my allowance. It's a great reward for doing your chores and getting good grades. Allowance is also good because it teaches you the value of money."

—Nicole

"I get an allowance of $10 a week. I have to pay for my own clothes. That has taught me a lot about responsibility."

—Joley

"My dad gives my brother and me $12 for allowance. Then he makes us pay $4 for 'taxes.' Another $4 goes toward savings. The last $4 we get to keep. So you could say that when all of our 'bills' are paid, we get $4."
—Jessica
"Kids should do chores around the house but not for an allowance. Our parents cook, clean, and drive us to school. The least we can do is help out a little without asking for money."
—Kelly
"I do not get an allowance. I don't ask for one because my parents buy me everything. If I want to go to the movies, my parents give me the money."
—Alexis
"Allowance should be a privilege, not a right. Kids should do something for their allowance."
—Jesek
10¢
5¢
25¢
25¢
10
1¢
1¢
1¢
5
5¢
1¢
25¢

CALENDAR
$
1
2
walk dog
3
4
water plants
5
6
take out trash
7
8
9
10
11
clean room
12
13
14
15
dishes
16
17
18
19
20
21
22
wash car
23
24
sweep
26
27
28
29
30
31

how to get a raise

Do you think you should get more allowance? How you talk to your parents will be key.

★ Pick a good time to talk. If your dad is talking on the phone and trying to feed peas to the baby, that is not the moment to march in and make your case.

★ Don't rely on comparisons. If you get 50¢ and every girl you know gets $5, OK—you can point that out. But if you get $5 and you've got a friend who gets $8, save your breath. Most parents want to use their own judgment—not the neighbors'.

★ Say you'll do extra work around the house. If it's your job to sweep the kitchen after dinner, offer to load the dishwasher, too. If you give more, you may get more.

★ Say you'll pay for more of your expenses. Your parents might think it's a good deal if you start paying for your own movies and treats.

★ Show your parents that you're responsible with the money you already have. Most adults are going to feel better about giving money to a girl who saves a third of her allowance than to a girl who blows her entire wad at the mall every payday.

★ Accept no for an answer. Your family's financial situation could make it impossible for your parents to give you more in allowance. Your parents also might just disagree with you about what the right amount should be. Either way, if you keep your cool and accept their decision with good grace, it could help you a year from now when you ask again. For now, turn your mind to ways to make money on your own.

Dear American Girl,
I'm starting middle school and I'm completely scared. It's going to be so different from elementary school. How am I going to survive?
—Scared

fresh start

Starting middle school might feel like the scariest thing in the world to you right now. But try to think of middle school as an awesome opportunity. New teachers and new kids mean you can arrive on the first day a new you! Have you always wanted to grow out your bangs? Do you think you look more like a Katharine than a Katie? Did you ever want to learn to write poetry? Now's your chance. You can change your style, change your favorite subject, or maybe just change your attitude.

Making new friends and branching out from the same kids you've played with since kindergarten isn't such a bad thing. It's like breaking in a new pair of shoes. They might feel a little uncomfortable at first, but after a while they'll feel great!

Quiz

how do you deal?

Middle school is all about change—new school, new teachers, new friends. How you cope with change will tell you a lot about how you'll adjust to your new surroundings. Choose the answer below that describes you best to see how you'll deal when it's for real.

1. This is the first year you have to take the bus to and from school. When you find this out, you . . .

   a. beg your dad to ask his boss to let him leave early every day to pick you up.

   b. call around to see if any other friends will be on your bus. Maybe you can sit together.

2. When your favorite teacher goes on maternity leave and is replaced with a substitute for the rest of the school year, you . . .

   a. find yourself saying, "That's not how Ms. Cho did it."

   b. help bring the new teacher up to speed on where Ms. Cho left off, and then let her do her own thing.

3. When you find out that none of your friends are in your classes this year, you . . .

   a. ask the guidance counselor to change your schedule so that you can be with your friends.

   b. feel bummed, but talk yourself into braving it alone.

4. Your brother says you'll have only three minutes to get from one class to another in middle school. You . . .

   a. gasp, "No way! I'll never make it."

   b. set a timer for three minutes to see just how long you'll have between classes.

5. Your best friend starts hanging out with a new girl at school. You . . .

   a. get jealous and give your friend the cold shoulder, hoping she'll get the hint that you don't like what she's doing.

   b. try to get to know the new girl. Maybe she'll turn out to be a great friend for you, too!

6. Your soccer coach scratches you from the starting lineup. You . . .

   a. sulk over to the bench and decide that soccer isn't your thing.

   b. stay on the sidelines and cheer the team on. If you pick up some good tips from the game, you might be able to earn back your position.

If you answered

Mostly a's

You're a holdout.
When change happens to you, you try to hang on to the way things used to be. Why? Because you know what to expect and what to do. You feel in control. But now that something new has come along, you're afraid you've lost control. **Don't be so quick to run.** New faces, places, and challenges can open up a whole new world for you. **And there is something you'll always have control over: how you handle and react to things.** As the unknown becomes more familiar, you'll find yourself feeling more sure of yourself.

Mostly b's

You like to go with the flow.
When faced with a big change, you take a deep breath and do your best. You know that nothing ever stays the same, and it's up to you to make the most of what's to come. Since you'll be making more of your own decisions in middle school, **it's important to keep your wits about you.** You'll have more responsibility and learn to manage more things on your own, which can make you feel really grown-up and make your parents proud of you.

Picture yourself having a good time in middle school.

Positive visualization is a trick that professional athletes use all the time. If you want to do well in a given situation, you have to want it, feel it, see it. That's not to say that you can close your eyes and imagine success one time and it will come. But it's a start! If you tell yourself you can do something, you've taken the first step toward making it a reality.

"what do I wear?"

A well-organized wardrobe can make a big difference when you're getting ready for school in a hurry. Follow these tips to get out the door feeling dressed for success.

★ **Clean clothes.** Make sure you have five or six outfits that you like to wear. That way, you'll have to do laundry just once a week and you'll have something clean for each day of the school week.

★ **Mix & match separates.** Buying clothes in basic colors makes it easier to create lots of different outfits. Make your style your own by adding jewelry, hair thingies, and other accessories.

★ **Clean out your closet.** Get rid of clothes that are too small by donating them to charity.

★ **Layers.** Layers allow you to adjust to the temperature throughout the day. You can tie a sweatshirt around your waist if you get warm.

★ **A clock.** A must-have for every middle schooler is a way to keep track of time, whether it's on your electronic device or on your wrist.

★ **Comfy shoes.** You need one pair for school and one for gym. Also have a pair in your closet for dressing up for the band concert.

★ **Crack the code.** Check your school's dress code and make sure the clothes you plan to wear are appropriate.

getting there

What if I oversleep and get to school late? Will I get into big trouble?
—Sleepy Samara

If you know you're going to be late, ask your mom or dad to write a note or call the school explaining why. It's OK to be tardy once in a while if you have a good reason. By middle school, though, you're expected to be there before the bell rings. If oversleeping is a problem for you, this is a good time to start working on new habits.

Last school year, I was late almost every day. Next year I am going to middle school, and I'll have to get up even earlier. I need a plan to help me get ready in the morning. Help!
—Not OK

Take a look at your morning schedule and see where you can gain some time. Do you need to set the alarm to go off earlier? Or maybe you should talk to your siblings about letting you in the bathroom first. Try some of the organization tips on the next page to get yourself up and out in the morning.

get into the habit

Make busy school days a bit easier by sticking to a **basic routine.** Doing tasks in the same order each day will help you remember what needs to be done. After a while, you'll whip through your routine in no time.

The night before

★ **Look at your planner or calendar** to see what the next day's schedule holds for you. Make any special arrangements and set out anything extra you'll need. For example, put out your flute if tomorrow's a band day.

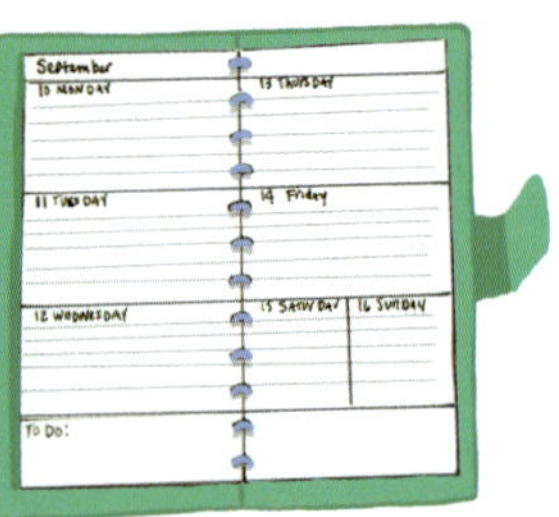

★ Set out or at least **think about what you're going to wear** the next day. Is your outfit clean?

★ **Pack your backpack** or book bag so that you can just grab it and go in the morning. **Homework done?**

★ Ask a parent to **sign any papers** or write any notes you need for the next day.

★ Pack your lunch or, if you need it, tuck **lunch money** into your backpack or book bag.

★ If you like to sleep in, **take a shower or bath at night** so that you'll be fresh for the coming day.

★ **Tuck in with a good book** to help you relax and get into dream mode.

The morning rush hour

- ★ **Stretch!**
- ★ Bathe or shower if you didn't the night before. If you did, just **freshen up quickly** in the bathroom.
- ★ **Get dressed.**
- ★ **Eat breakfast**—preferably sitting down!
- ★ Do a **quick mirror check** to make sure your hair is neat and your shirt isn't inside out.
- ★ **Grab** your stuff **and go.**

Breakfast Bets

Everyone knows it's really important to have breakfast every morning. But did you know that some breakfasts can leave you tired and sluggish around mid-morning? Foods high in processed sugars and flour, such as sweetened cereals and frosted toaster pastries, can actually zap your energy. Whole-grain foods, fruits, and protein will keep you going. Some energizing choices are whole-wheat toast with peanut butter, granola, an apple or banana, yogurt, oatmeal, or a glass of milk.

before you go

Even more important than school supplies and new shoes is bringing a good attitude with you as you head to middle school.

Be self-confident.

Almost every girl cares what other people think about her—especially when meeting new classmates or trying out a new look. **It's natural to be a little unsure of yourself** in new situations, but try not to think the worst when things are left unsaid. If someone is staring at your new haircut, she may be thinking how it would look on her!

Be realistic.

You skipped over question #3 on the test and blew your chance for a perfect score. So you spend the rest of the day thinking: *How could I be so stupid?* **Give yourself a break.** Don't beat yourself up over every little mistake. Instead, celebrate what you did right, and accept and understand what you did wrong. Then move on, knowing that you did the best you could do.

Be levelheaded.

Worrying sucks up your energy. Don't let thoughts about what could go wrong eat away at your precious time, or you'll be left with nothing to show for it—except a bellyful of butterflies. Focus on what good things could happen: *I might get an A!* If you have to consider the negative "what-ifs," follow up each one with a positive "what-if." Give yourself five minutes; then **get on with things.**

Be open-minded.

Much of your time in middle school is spent getting tested, graded, and evaluated. Teacher comments, class critics, and even input from parents can sometimes hurt. Try to take each comment one at a time and see if you can use the advice that's given. **Don't take it personally or get discouraged.** Remind yourself:

Don't worry—you'll be just fine. Soon enough, **YOU** could be giving advice to someone else who is scared about starting middle school, just like you were.

I love so many sports! I like ballet, jazz, and tap because I get to dance my heart out. I like soccer because it gives me a chance to run in the green grass. I like tennis because it's good exercise and it makes me feel alive. And I like volleyball because it feels so great to hit that ball!

—Alisson

play power

what's so great about sports?

You like playing a sport—or doing something that works your body and keeps you fit. So why do you do it?

Maybe you play because you love to run, shoot hoops, kick a ball, or do back handsprings—because it just feels great!

Maybe you think *any* kind of moving is more fun than sitting still or staring at a screen.

Maybe you like discovering your body can do things you didn't know it could do.

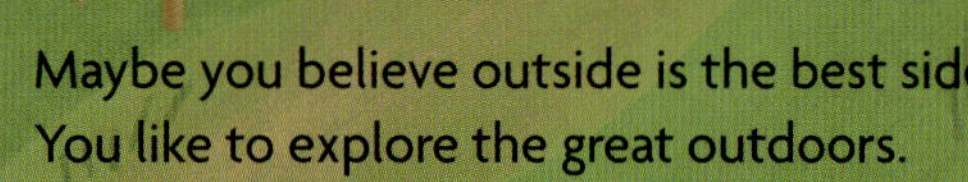

Maybe you believe outside is the best side! You like to explore the great outdoors.

Maybe you play sports because you like being part of a team . . .

. . . or because it's fun hanging out with your teammates. *Hellooo,* pizza parties!

. . . or because the feeling you get when your team accomplishes something together is like happy-times-10!

High five!
Those are all great reasons. And that's not even all you get when you play.

IMPORTANT!

Before doing any of the exercises described or shown in this book, check with your parent, coach, doctor, or other appropriate adult to make sure it's right for you, your body, and your sport.

body bonuses

You play because it's fun! But that's not all. Playing sports also sets you up to be healthier for your whole life.

It helps your bones.

Bones are made of living cells. When you do weight-bearing exercise, new bone tissue is formed, and that makes your bones stronger. Any sport is weight-bearing if your legs support your body weight while you move. So when you're walking, running, jumping rope, dancing, or playing soccer or basketball, you're building strong bones.

It helps your muscles.

Well, duh, right? If you play sports, your muscles get stronger. That's Sports 101. But what does that really mean? It means you don't get tired as quickly when you play. And the stronger your muscles are, the better they are at protecting you when you're moving. That means you're less prone to certain types of injuries, both on and off the field.

It helps your heart.

Exercise that gets your heart pumping and makes you breathe hard is giving your heart a workout, too. Your heart is a muscle. And the stronger it is, the better it is at pumping blood to your lungs and the rest of your body. More oxygen and nutrients get to your tissues. You're heart-healthier, and you have more energy.

It helps your ZZZs.

This one's simple. Experts who study fitness say exercise can help you sleep better, and a well-rested you is a happier, healthier you.

How much exercise do I need?

Health experts say girls your age should get at least an hour of physical activity every day. If you play sports, practicing and competing will get you to an hour on many days. Gym class counts, too. So does recess and walking the dog.

As part of that activity, you should do something that gets your heart pumping for at least 30 minutes three times a week. Those 30 minutes can be two 15-minute or three 10-minute bursts of activity. You'll get the same health benefits as an all-at-once 30-minute workout.

What kind of exercise is best? Anything that's so fun it makes you want to play! In fact, experts who study fitness recommend that you don't pick just one sport to specialize in. Playing multiple sports is best for your body.

It helps your future.

You haven't met Grown-Up You yet. But if you keep playing sports, you're going to like her when you do. Not only will Grown-Up You be fun to hang around with, she'll also be healthy and fit. Playing sports now means you're more likely to be active as an adult.

brain bonuses

You play because it feels good—starting with the thrill of the game. But sports and exercise also feel good in ways that might not seem so obvious.

MORE *self-confidence*

When you have fun playing a sport, you feel good about yourself. Whether you're scoring the goal, making a solid pass, or cheering from the sidelines, mastering a skill makes you proud. It can help you realize you're capable of doing other amazing things, too.

LESS *stress*

Does it seem weird that playing in a real nail-biter or doing a hard workout can reduce your stress? It's science! It happens because exercise can reduce the levels of hormones in your body that are related to stress, such as *adrenaline.*

BETTER *moods*

Exercise stimulates the production of brain chemicals called *endorphins.* Endorphins are known as "mood elevators" because they can help you feel happy, optimistic, and less depressed. It's like pushing a button for your brain to take an elevator to a happier floor. It's the science behind why a walk, swim, or bike ride can get you feeling up.

BETTER *concentration*

Remember how your pumping heart is increasing the blood flow throughout your body? The blood is pumping to your brain, too, and that can make your brain function better. Some research shows that exercise activates the *hippocampus*, the part of your brain that's important for memory and learning.

IMPROVED *performance at school*

Researchers have found that girls who play sports often do better academically. And because you're sleeping better and concentrating better, you may also, in turn, be getting better grades.

MORE *time to chill*

Some exercise helps you relax because of the kind of activity you're doing. Maybe you like the solitude of walking the dog or the peace of canoeing with your big sister on a quiet lake. Some people get their best thinking done when they have fewer distractions. Worries about friend drama, school, or your busy schedule just fade away. *Ahhh!* Peace and quiet, inside and out.

life bonuses

You play sports because you like to! It feels good to play, but more than that, you're picking up skills that can help you off the field, too—now and for the rest of your life.

You learn that you can deal with life's ups and downs.

In sports, you know you may win . . . or lose. You keep going, even if it's hard. That's called *perseverance*. You learn to look back at a loss and find things about your performance that were "wins." Knowing that who you are is not decided by what happens during one event can help you at school, at home, or at work someday.

Being able to bounce back when things don't turn out as you'd hoped—that's called *resilience*. It makes it easier to deal with new situations and bumps in the road your whole life. You know that the challenge might be easy—or not—but either way, you can keep moving forward.

You learn people skills.

In sports, you play with loud people, quiet people, goofballs, and serious types. You learn how to cheer them on and support them if they're down. You learn that if you speak up when you don't understand, things will make more sense. You learn there are good ways and bad ways to disagree.

Being able to empathize and being good at communicating and resolving conflicts will make you stronger and more independent wherever you go. These skills make you a leader!

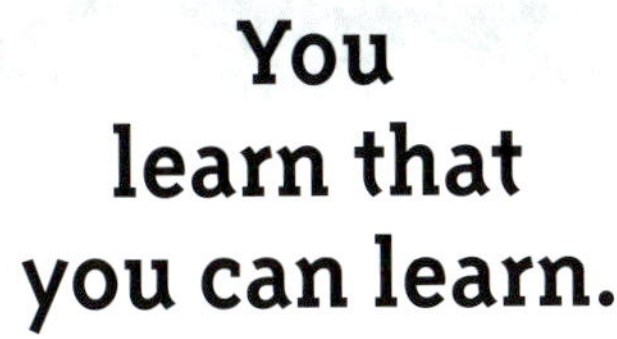

You learn that you can learn.

Picture yourself playing your favorite sport. You may not remember, but there was a day when you'd never played it before. You had never, say, kicked a soccer ball—ever. But look at you now: You have skills! You learned a few things and then a few more. You're still improving. Throughout your life, you'll always need to learn—whether it's skills for your career . . .

I need to fix this Mars Rover, stat!

. . . or to understand what's going on in the world and solve problems.

As president of the United States, here's what I think . . .

As an athlete, you understand it's OK not to know everything at first, because you can learn. That translates to confidence and bravery.

You learn to handle pressure situations.

Races, games, matches—in sports, competition can equal excitement. There are bound to be pressure-filled situations, like when your team is down by one in the ninth inning and you're up to bat.

In solo sports you take on pressure, too. Imagine you're surfing: You see the perfect wave forming, and you're trying to position yourself to catch it before it's gone. You learn it can be fun to conquer a challenge.

That doesn't mean you'll never be worried or nervous. You learn to recognize nerves, take a deep breath, and face the task head-on. And a girl who's ready to face a challenge with gusto instead of fear will go far.

Quiz

why do you play?

Stop and think for a minute about why you like to play sports, whether it's a team activity or something you do on your own. Which of these sound most like you? Pick all the answers that apply.

I like to go all out!

Playing in games is exciting!

My teammates are my best friends.

I found out I'm good at this, and I can accomplish things.

It takes my mind off other things. When I play, I focus on the game and everything else goes away.

My sisters all play volleyball, so I do it, too.

I like that I get more time with my friends.

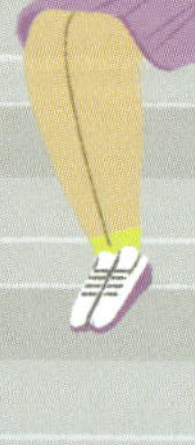

It makes me feel graceful and creative.

I love being outside.

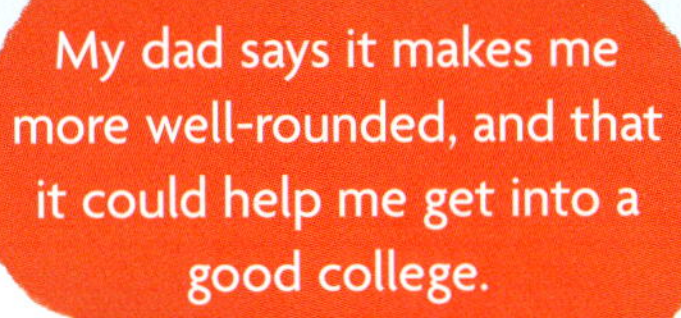

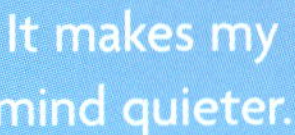

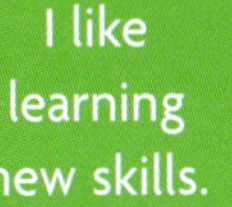

Scoreboard

You may play because it's **fun** or because it makes you **feel good.** You may play because it **strengthens your friendships** or because you **find out new things** about yourself along the way.

If your answers show you might be playing for **reasons that aren't your own,** dig deeper. Can you think of two or three things you enjoy about playing? Did it take a tiny push to get you started, but you like it now? How often do you come home from practice or a game with a smile on your face? If you can't come up with positive answers to these questions, this book will help you find a solution—or find the fun!

WHAT'S IN YOUR SUITCASE?

be prepared

A fun part of travel is the prepping and planning beforehand.

What should I bring?

2-WAY RETURN TICKET

How will we get there?

SEAT 13B 14:15

VALID NOW = ROUTE ANYWHERE

What will we do?

COLETTE INN

HOW CAN WE ASSIST YOU?

Where will we stay?

What will we eat?

make an itinerary

An itinerary is a list of what you want to do on your trip. As a family, you can gather ideas by researching on the Internet or checking out travel books from the library. Make a giant list of all the cool things you could do and then narrow it down. You don't want to overplan, or you'll end up exhausted and stressed out. Leave some time to just wander around. And make sure everyone in the family gets to see or do at least one thing that excites them.

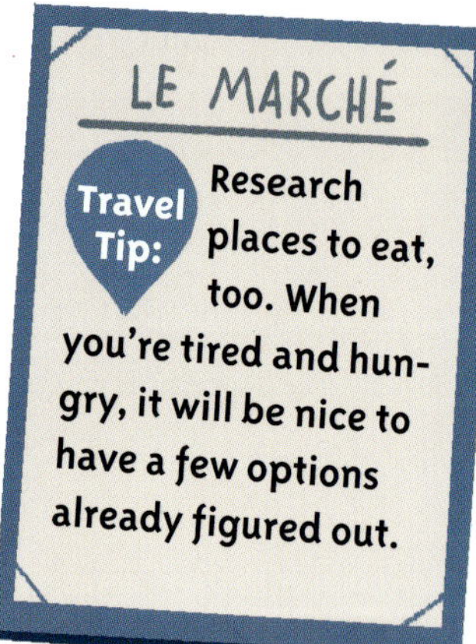

If you're leaving the country

An international trip takes a little bit more preparation. In addition to creating an itinerary, your family might want to do some extra research to learn about the food, language, and weather.

If you're traveling to a country where the people speak another language, explore the language resources at the library or download a basic language app with your parent's permission. Learning how to say hello, good-bye, please, and thank you can be really helpful.

If you're concerned about the food, try the country's cuisine at a local restaurant so you'll get an idea of what you might like. No matter where you travel in the world, you can usually find unique sandwiches, noodle and rice dishes, soups, and pastries.

Do you need a passport?

If you're traveling outside the United States, you'll need a passport. Even babies need passports! A passport is an official document with your photo and personal information. It allows the government to protect you while you travel to another country.

Wondering why your passport is a booklet with blank pages? It's for stamps. Each time you visit another country, you'll get a new stamp when you enter and sometimes when you leave. The stamp usually includes the date, and it means that you have been approved to visit the country for a certain amount of time.

how to pack

Packing is a skill that you'll get better at with practice. Start thinking about what you need a week before you leave.

Don't overpack

Packing light means you'll only bring the essentials. When you pack light, you can carry your own stuff, keep track of it, and easily unpack and repack it. Think about what you will actually want to wear and use each day.

What do you need for a seven-day trip?

- 7 pairs of underwear (and socks if needed)
- 2 pairs of shoes (so you can alternate if your feet hurt)
- 2–3 bottoms such as pants, shorts, or skirts
- 5–7 tops such as tank tops or T-shirts
- A jacket, sweater, or scarf to keep you warm on the plane or at night
- 1–2 sets of pajamas
- A reusable bag (for dirty clothes, souvenirs, or to use as a day bag)
- Optional: a swimsuit, snow pants, a fancy dress, or whatever else you'll need that's specific to your trip

Travel Tip: If you aren't positive that you'll use something during your trip, don't bring it "just in case." You can usually buy it once you get there if you really need it.

Travel Tip: Check the weather forecast for your destination before you pack.

get coordinated

Pack complete outfits that already match and are ready to wear. In fact, pack some of your favorite outfits that fit well and make you feel great. (Packing a brand-new outfit isn't a good idea. What if it ends up being uncomfortable?) If you pack clothing and accessories that are in the same color family, you can easily mix and match them during your trip to create even more outfits.

Travel Tip:

Layering with a cardigan or scarf can help you create even more outfits when matched with different tops. A scarf can double as a light blanket, too.

Don't forget the toiletries

You'll need toothpaste and a toothbrush, plus a hairbrush or comb and a few of your favorite hair accessories. Most hotels have soap, shampoo, conditioner, lotion, and a hair dryer. Put all toiletries in plastic zip-top bags so they don't leak.

Something extra

When you travel, you won't have a lot of the comforts from your home. But a small pillow, night-light, or stuffed animal may make you feel a little more comfortable and help you sleep better.

Fold or roll?

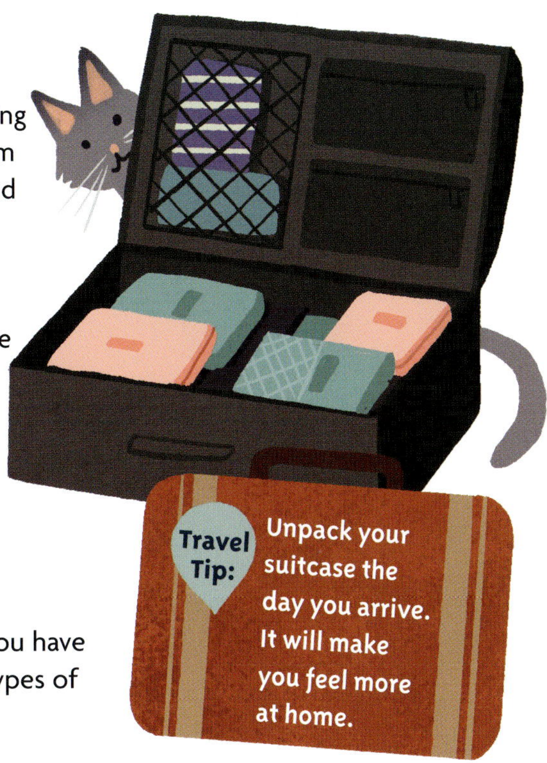

Some travelers swear that rolling clothes instead of folding them saves room in your suitcase and makes clothing less wrinkly. Try both ways and see what you think. Here's another tip worth trying: Packing cubes are zippered compartments that can help keep your clothing organized and keep clean and dirty clothes separate during your trip.

Luggage lingo

If you're flying somewhere, you have the option of bringing two types of bags to the airport.

Carry-on

A carry-on bag is small enough to fit underneath the airplane seat in front of you or above your seat in the overhead compartment. Carry-on bags are perfect for snacks, a book, and headphones. You'll have to carry this bag around the airport and through the security lines so make sure it's not too heavy, and make sure it zips or buckles on top so things don't fall out.

Checked bag

A checked bag is a larger piece of luggage that's given to the airline when you first check in at the airport. The airline makes sure your bag gets onto the correct plane. Checked bags are stored in the cargo compartment in the bottom of the plane during the flight. When you arrive, the bags are brought to the baggage claim area, where passengers pick them up. Most people pack their clothes, shoes, and toiletries in checked bags.

getting there

How you travel to your destination is part of the fun.

Look up! At any moment, there are about 10,000 planes in the air.

PATAGONIA
APR 2 2010

Route 66 is a famous highway that travels through eight states from Chicago, Illinois, to Santa Monica, California. It's a favorite road trip for many families!

Some cruise ships travel around the entire world! It takes more than 100 days to complete the trip.

It takes 51 hours—one way—for the California Zephyr to travel from Chicago to San Francisco.

SINGLE PASSENGER

NYC→BOS

You can take a bus up and down the East Coast and see cities such as Charleston, Philadelphia, and Boston along the way.

BUS TICKET

It would take 40 hours to drive nonstop from Washington, D.C., to San Francisco.

at the airport

Airports are busy, busy, busy! There are so many people coming and going, traveling near and traveling far. The airports in Atlanta, Chicago, and Los Angeles are among the busiest in the world.

You need to be extra cautious when you're at any airport. You have to keep track of your belongings, stay out of everyone's way, and follow the rules very carefully.

1. Arrive early: two hours before your flight, or three hours early if you are leaving the country.

2. Check in. Your family can do this online or at the counter at the airport. You'll get a boarding pass with a seat number.

3. Check your large bags at the counter. Bring your carry-on bag with you.

4. Go through the security checkpoint.

5. Walk to your gate (check the big "departures" monitors if your gate number isn't listed on your boarding pass).

6. Go to the bathroom, fill up your water bottle, and get some snacks. Now wait patiently to board the plane.

Flying is fun

Riding in an airplane is such a cool experience. You're super high up in the air and you're traveling super fast. The views are awesome! And once you land, you're in a totally new place. How amazing is that?

Some people do get a little nervous on planes. Planes make a lot of noises, and sometimes there are bumps in the air—just like there are when a car drives over a bumpy road. If you get scared on the plane, just remember that the pilots will do everything they can to keep you safe. It's actually safer to ride in a plane than it is to ride in a car.

To calm your nerves, try closing the window shade, listening to music, reading a book, doing a crossword puzzle, or watching a movie. Or close your eyes and slowly breathe in and out ten times. You'll be there before you know it.

Flying alone?

Kids between ages 5 and 15 can fly alone as "unaccompanied minors." An airline representative will make sure you never walk alone in the airport, and they won't leave your side until you meet your family member at your destination. Listen carefully to directions, hang on to your travel documents, and you'll be fine!

boredom busters

Whether you're in a bus, on a plane, on a train, or in a car, it's likely you'll have more than a few hours of time on your hands.

Conversation starters

Use this together time as a chance to really get to know your family. Write a list of questions that you can ask every member of your family. Some suggestions to get you started: What is your favorite food? What is your best memory? Where would you live if you could live anywhere in the world?

Who am I?

On scraps of paper or note cards, ask your family to write down famous people or characters. Collect the papers and mix them up. Now let one family member draw a name (but don't show it to anyone else). The other family members can ask yes-or-no questions to try to figure out who it is.

Scavenger hunt

Ask your family to help you create a list of items that you might see in the airport or on the road. Or try to find one item for each letter of the alphabet. See if you can cross everything off the list before you arrive at your destination.

Easy things to pack:

Notebook and colored pencils

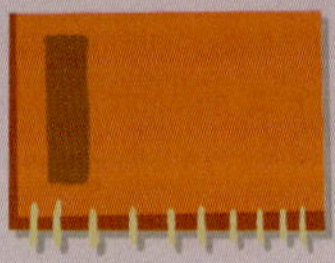

Puzzle book

Magazine or book

Handheld video game

Coloring book

Card game

Music player and headphones

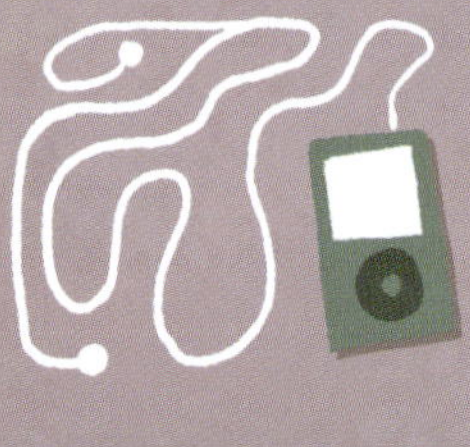

Journal and pen

Snacks for the road

Whenever you're traveling, it's good to have some snacks on hand. Travel plans don't always go perfectly, so it's possible that you could end up very hungry with no food in sight. Here are some snacks that are easy to travel with. Store them in zip-top bags.

Fresh fruit: grapes, strawberries, and orange slices

Trail mix: dry cereal, dried fruit, popcorn, pretzels, and chocolate pieces

Sandwich squares: cut a sandwich into quarters

Veggie mix: carrot sticks, cucumber slices, and cherry tomatoes

Cheese and crackers: string cheese or slices of cheese and whole-grain crackers

smart girl's GUIDE
American Girl
COOKING
how to make food for
your friends, your family & yourself

Food
glorious
Food

join the club

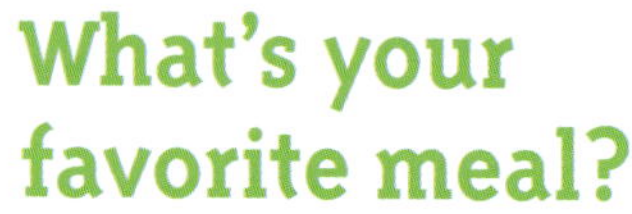

Turkey, stuffing, and all the trimmings at Thanksgiving?

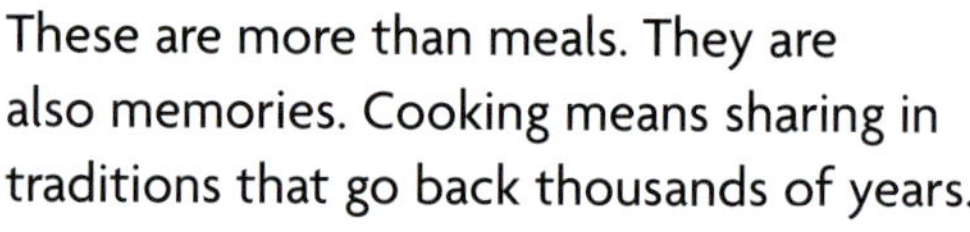

These are more than meals. They are also memories. Cooking means sharing in traditions that go back thousands of years.

Family recipes hold family history. Maybe your great-grandmother brought that pasta recipe with her from Rome. Maybe your dad learned to make his tacos in Texas when he was a kid. Wherever they came from, those recipes contain stories about your own past.

Cooking passes on world history, too. Every culture expresses itself with its own special foods. When you're eating hummus, spring rolls, or curry, you're experiencing other places in the tastiest way.

Adults Required!

A kitchen is a glorious place. It can also be a dangerous one, though. So before you do any of the activities in this book, ask permission from an adult. And while you're in the kitchen, an adult needs to be with you at all times. Never cook alone. (Cooking is more fun with other people anyway!)

You can join that great tradition. It's easy. Not only can you learn to make family favorites, but you can invent your own mouthwatering dishes, too.

The more you cook, the more you'll get to know how foods and flavors go together, and how to change things up the way you like. One day you won't even need a recipe—except when you want to try something really different.

Cooking is old, yet at the same time, for a creative cook, cooking is always new.

Welcome to the club!

family traditions

Do you and your family eat a special holiday meal, handed down for generations? Or do you have fun food traditions that you invented yourselves? Here's what girls have to share about their own family traditions.

Every year, my family and I—including my mom, sister, cousin, grandma, and aunts—make hundreds of homemade ravioli to eat at holidays and birthday dinners. They are the most delicious ravioli ever tasted, hands down!

—Rosita

For Hanukkah, my mom always makes her own donuts and potato pancakes.

—Rachel

At Christmas, my mama makes tamales and posole. Posole is a Mexican soup that has hominy, meat, and a spicy broth. Tamales have masa on the outside and spicy sauce and meat on the inside. They're delicious!

—Naya

I'm from Sweden, and we always make saffron buns for the holiday Saint Lucia. The buns are shaped like an S and have raisins. Saint Lucia brings light to the darkest time of the year!

—Caroline

We have spaghetti for dinner every Monday night. It always gives me something to look forward to on the first day of the school week!

—Katie

My family makes monkey bread for any special holiday. My mom makes it, my mom's mom makes it, and my mom's mom's mom makes it, too!

—Tyler

My grandma has a recipe called Czech puzzle cookies. They are crunchy and have powdered sugar all over them, and they're so good! Best of all, she passed the recipe down to my sister and me.

—Erin

For our tradition, my family always has a Sunday night dinner. I like it because this is a time every week when I get to be with my sister and brother, who are gone a lot. We always have a special home-cooked meal.

—Madelyn

About once a month, my mom or dad will serve one of us kids on a special bright red plate. When someone gets the special plate, each family member will say one good thing about him or her while we eat dinner.

—Eva

My family celebrates Eid. Girls wear clothes called *salwar kameez*, and everyone eats a rice dish called *biryani* and a dessert called *mitai*.

—Sania

the joys of cooking

What's so great about cooking? Let's see . . .

Cooking is fun!

It gives you a zillion chances to explore and experiment. Comb through cookbooks and websites for dishes that get you excited. Discover the foods of other countries and cultures. Be creative with flavors and food combinations. There's no end to the pleasures you'll find.

Cooking brings people together.

Sure, you can make something just for yourself. But cooking is a great way to have fun with friends and family. Put on some music and pull your pals into the kitchen. Decorate cupcakes. Create personal pizzas. Mash up guacamole. Take your place among the family's holiday cooks and show what you can do.

Cooking keeps you healthy and strong.

When you make your own meals, you're eating fresh food that you know is good, not mystery ingredients from plastic packages. If you're the cook, you're more likely to know what's really on your plate—and to care.

Cooking puts you in charge.

When you know how to make your own meals, you're the boss. You can design your own lunches. You can cook just what you like for friends. You don't have to rely on someone else. You're the chef!

Cooking is delicious.

Making—and eating—scrumptious homemade food is one of life's great pleasures. It just is.

your cooking sense

Which of these scenes describes you the best?

1. The French bread recipe calls for 1 tablespoon of sugar. You . . .

a. use a cereal spoon to add a heap of sugar to the mixing bowl.

b. add just enough sugar to fill up the cereal spoon, then dump the sugar into the bowl.

c. find the measuring spoon marked "1 T," fill it just to the rim, and add the sugar to the bowl.

2. You're supposed to "whisk" three eggs together. You . . .

a. crack the eggs into a bowl and use a cooking tool with wire loops to stir them until they're frothy.

b. crack the eggs into a bowl and blend them briskly (rhymes with *whiskly*) with a wooden spoon.

c. put three eggs in a bowl and hope for the best.

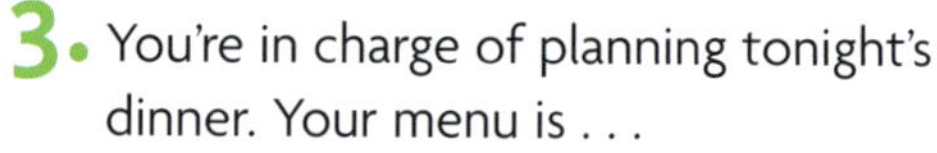

3. You're in charge of planning tonight's dinner. Your menu is . . .

a. rice, French fries, pizza, and mashed potatoes, because everybody loves those, right?

b. roast chicken, rice pilaf, and a big green salad.

c. something easy—maybe chicken nuggets and brownies?

4. It's time to start making your dad's favorite vegetable soup. The first thing you do is . . .

a. read the first step in the recipe and do what it says: Add carrots to the pot.

b. read the whole recipe, including the ingredients list, and realize that you have to peel and chop the carrots first. You do that and add them to the pot.

c. read the whole recipe, including the ingredients list. Then you measure, peel, and chop everything and have all the ingredients ready before you start cooking.

5. The cake batter is in the pans and ready to bake. You . . .

a. slide the pans into the heated oven and leave the kitchen. You'll remember to take them out. Probably.

b. slide the pans into the heated oven, set the timer, take out the pans to cool when they're done, and turn off the oven.

c. slide the pans into the heated oven, set the timer, and turn off the oven when they're done, leaving the pans in there. They'll stay nice and warm.

6. It's time for your morning smoothie. You . . .

a. make the same banana smoothie as always. Why mess with success?

b. read through a cookbook and decide you'll take a chance on a blueberry smoothie soon.

c. invent something new—new fruits, new yogurts, new combinations—every week!

Answers

1. If you chose **c,** you already know the difference between spoons used for measuring and spoons used for eating or stirring. Measuring spoons (and measuring cups) allow you to add exactly the right amount of an ingredient to a recipe. When you're baking something like bread or cake or cookies, it's especially important that measurements are precise. That's because the ingredients that make baked things deliciously puffy or chewy have to be in just the right amount to do their job. It's chemistry in action!

2. If you chose **a,** you know there are special tools and techniques for mixing ingredients together. A whisk is an actual gadget that's used to whip ingredients by hand when a spoon won't do. With a whisk, you can add air to eggs so they're light and fluffy, or mix oil and vinegar together into a creamy salad dressing, or make thick whipped cream from the liquid in the carton.

3. If you chose **b,** you have a good sense of what makes a meal both exciting and healthy. When planning a meal, cooks decide which foods from different food groups they'll include. (That's the healthy part.) They also think about ways to make a meal look yummy on the plate, such as combining colors and serving a pleasing variety of foods.

4. If you chose **c,** you realize that the best way to follow a recipe is to read it all the way through ***before*** you start cooking. Then you won't have any surprises. ***("What? I was supposed to turn the oven on??")*** Also, it gives you a chance to prepare your ingredients and have them ready so that you can time things right during the cooking part.

5. If you chose **b,** you probably have some experience with a regular oven. You know that when you turn the oven off, it stays hot for a while, so any food still in there will keep cooking. (A microwave oven, on the other hand, stops cooking the instant it turns off.)

6. If you chose **a, b,** or **c,** it's all good! Whether you love sticking with familiar favorites or trying new creations every day, making food is all about expressing yourself and discovering what you like.

Want more information on a topic in this book? Collect all the Smart Girl's Guides! Visit your favorite bookseller or go to www.americangirl.com.

- ☐ Smart Girl's Guide to Cooking
- ☐ Smart Girl's Guide to Crushes
- ☐ Smart Girl's Guide to Drama, Rumors, & Secrets
- ☐ Smart Girl's Guide to Friendship Troubles

- ☐ Smart Girl's Guide to Getting It Together
- ☐ Smart Girl's Guide to Knowing What to Say
- ☐ Smart Girl's Guide to Liking Herself

- ☐ Smart Girl's Guide to Making a Difference
- ☐ Smart Girl's Guide to Manners
- ☐ Smart Girl's Guide to Middle School
- ☐ Smart Girl's Guide to Money
- ☐ Smart Girl's Guide to Race & Inclusion
- ☐ Smart Girl's Guide to Sports & Fitness
- ☐ Smart Girl's Guide to Travel
- ☐ Smart Girl's Guide to Understanding Families
- ☐ Smart Girl's Guide to Worry